Against All Odds:
A Success Story

CHARLTON MAXWELL JIMERSON

ISBN: 1496156412
ISBN 13: 9781496156419
Library of Congress Control Number: 2014910133
CreateSpace Independent Publishing Platform
North Charleston, South Carolina

Charlton Maxwell Jimerson is a Major League Baseball outfielder who was born in San Leandro, California, in 1979. He survived a turbulent childhood, saved in part by discovering his love of baseball at an early age. He was drafted out of high school in the twenty-fourth round of the 1997 Major League Baseball Amateur draft, but he chose to put his education first and attended the University of Miami, Florida. As a Miami Hurricane, Jimerson won two NCAA Collegiate Baseball National Championships and was named the 2001 College World Series Most Outstanding Player.

After college, Jimerson went on to play in the Minor Leagues. *Baseball America* reported him as having the "Best Outfield Arm," as well as being the "Best Athlete" in the Houston Astros farm system in 2005. Later that year, Jimerson made his Major League debut with the Houston Astros on September 14th, 2005. Under the tutelage of the Major League Baseball Hall of Fame player Tony Gwynn, Jimerson began to understand the "sweet science" of hitting a baseball. Oddly, Jimerson had to wait until 2006 to get his first at-bat in the Major Leagues. That's when Jimerson pinch-hit for Roger Clemens, belting a home run his first at-bat.

"You never know how strong you can be, until being strong is the only choice you have left."
-Tupac Shakur

1ST INNING:

Where did my memory go? I mean, I'm sure I had plenty of joyful moments as a child to reflect on, but I can't seem to recall many. I know they must exist because at times in my life, the simplest things could spark the fire that fuels my memory engine. Something as simple as hearing a song on the radio, or seeing a familiar face, can catapult my mind and body into feeling like déjà vu. But for the life of me, I can't seem to locate some of my childhood's most intimate experiences. I often fail to recollect milestone events in my life, like my first day of school, or the first time I kissed a girl. Some say my inability to reminiscence is my defense mechanism—not retaining information subconsciously due to the trauma many of the events caused me. Therefore, if I can't remember it, then it must not have happened. Guess I can't argue with those who have studied psychology and know me best. Nonetheless, I have never forgotten where I came from and the trials and tribulations that helped shape me as a man. A memoir is defined as a record of events written by a person having intimate knowledge of them based on personal observation. These are my memories based on my observation, and nobody can tell my story better than I can.

I came into this world with a strong grip on the doctors' two index fingers as he lifted me away from my mother's hospital bed. If only taking hold of my own life after that autumn day was just as easy. Born on the morning of September 22nd, 1979, weighing seven pounds and eight ounces, I had no idea that I was born into a generational curse of anger, addiction, and misfortune. My father Eugene was a strong-willed and aggressive man by nature; yet he possessed a sensitive and emotional side that he often had difficulty expressing. As a former standout wrestler at Oakland High, my father kept an athletic build. During the time when I was born, my father often associated himself with members of the Black Panther Party. Though he shared a mutual rebellious attitude with the Black Panthers, he wasn't prepared to go to jail or die for the cause. My father was a people's person at heart. He paraded the streets of Oakland like the mayor, shaking hands and kissing babies. He loved horses and you could often catch him at Golden Gate Fields in Berkeley, California, betting the $2 trifecta on a race. My mother Charlene—with her tall, petite frame and dark skin—was a rebel in her own right. She always knew what she wanted to do, when she would do it, and no one could tell her otherwise. Like most women, her power was packed in her tongue. Since she couldn't match my father's size and strength, my mother would verbally attack Eugene with nasty words. My father would often respond by physically abusing Charlene, sometimes even while she was pregnant with me. When I got older, my mother made sure that I was aware of the physical abuse my father subjected her to. I believe she never wanted me to forget all that she had went through to give me life.

While my parents eagerly awaited my return from the newborn nursery, a nurse asked my father what my name would be. Eugene replied, "Charlton.... Charlton Maxwell Jimerson!" He said it with so much pride and happiness that the people in the room couldn't help but share his joy. My first name was derived from my mother's name Charlene. Although the two names don't phonetically sound alike, the only difference in spelling is the last three letters. My middle name came from the Maxwell House brand of coffee my father preferred to drink. My father was so proud of my middle name that he always reminded me to include it on every document. He later expressed to me how he enjoyed the *wow* response he received when he told people what my full name was. It was a name constructed to exude intelligence and demand respect, even before you met me. Surely, based on what he had witnessed in America, my father knew that a name could be a hindrance if it sounds too *ghetto*. Names like Tyrone and Desean are just what racists and bigots are looking for on applications so they can immediately place them in the circular file. Qualifications listed on a resume hold no value if human resources don't look past the name at the top of the paper. My name was specifically formulated to prevent those acts of prejudgment and discrimination, because on paper it was not obvious that I was Black.

My mother already had three children prior to my arrival. From oldest to youngest are my brothers Derell and Eugene Jr., and my only sister Lanette. Derell was conceived in between one of many relationship breaks between my mother and father. Derell's biological father proved to be just another dead beat who made a child he could not take care of. At that time, fatherless children were a growing epidemic in the Black community for several reasons. Mostly because of the rise of crack cocaine and the United States government's war against drugs. Increased jail time for possession of crack cocaine placed a lot of Black fathers behind bars for long sentences. Eugene Jr. was my father's pride and joy, hence why he was given my father's namesake. Though my father loved Derell unconditionally, Eugene Jr. was my father's prize production. Eugene Jr. was my father's first child that he could take ownership for bringing into this world. Two years later, a Jimerson baby girl was born. Lanette's status as the only girl amongst all boys would become extremely important later in life. Her position as next in line to be matriarch would be vital to my survival.

Being raised in the grimy streets of the San Francisco Bay Area, I learned early that only the strong survive in this urban melting pot. In the Bay, it is not unusual to see people from five or six different ethnic backgrounds in one classroom or workplace. Out west, people don't see color lines but rather an opportunity to share and experience different cultures and customs. In the early '80s, when I was just a toddler, people were spreading love and peace throughout Northern California. People of all races were also coming together to share in illegal activity. In free-spirited cities like Berkeley and San Francisco, everyone was using illicit drugs without restraint. Whether it was snorting cocaine or sharing needles, people were always looking for something to liven the party. In Oakland, cocaine was losing its luster and crack cocaine was on deck. Unfortunately, the latter blanketed the Jimerson family tree like a steady snowfall covers the pine trees in the winter.

Though my parents' relationship was rocky before I was born, my birth was a reason for them to try to work out their problems. Unfortunately, my father's uncontrolled anger and intense jealousy, combined with my mother's stubbornness, eventually caused them to split. All of the children stayed with my mother, while Eugene faded out of our lives in frustration. Though we remained in Oakland for most of my early childhood years, we changed addresses like a free agent athlete changes teams. We had problems everywhere we went in some form or fashion. Sometimes it was drug related, other times it was problems correlated to our environment. While living in the 'hood, many problems were unavoidable. Robbery, drive-by shootings, and assaults were common occurrences in our community. For example, while living in East Oakland, our home was burglarized and all my baby pictures were stolen. The burglars just snatched everything in sight out of blind greed, oblivious to the fact that their new possessions included my entire collection of childhood photos. Those photos were more than just images captured on chemically-enhanced paper. Those photos were the road map to journey back through my childhood memories. Unfortunately, those memories would be gone forever.

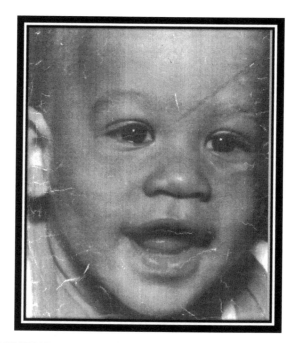

ONE OF FEW PICTURES OF MYSELF FROM MY EARLY CHILDHOOD

In 1986, my mother felt like we needed a change. A fresh start began when we moved twenty miles south to the city of Hayward. Historically, Hayward is primarily known for its temperate climate and fertile soil. In the 1950s, the city was a perfect location for farmers to raise cattle and chickens, or produce fruits like apricots and cherries. By the 1980s, Hayward had already expanded from a town of mainly local farmers, to a mixture of inner city and suburbia residents. Although it wasn't a very big city, it was a far cry from a small town. I didn't mind the move because as the days went on, life in Oaktown wasn't getting any better. The only thing that I would miss about Oakland was being close to my grandmother's house that I loved to visit. Besides the fact that it was the only Jimerson residence that remained unchanged, Grandma's house had character. The living room contained a plastic covered sofa and a rocking chair in the corner. Next to the window stood an art deco dresser with a record player inside and vinyl R&B records underneath. In the corner collecting dust was a large, bulky, black and white television with UHF and VHF channel knobs. A small dining room separated the living room from the wallpapered kitchen in the back. Granny's kitchen was always guaranteed to have iced lemon cake sitting in the shiny glass cake holder on the counter. No one could top Granny's iced lemon cake that I loved. My grandmother's skills in the kitchen was one of the reasons why my uncles still lived with her well into their adulthood. I believe that they never could find a woman that could compare to my grandmother.

We moved into a lovely three-bedroom home in downtown Hayward, oddly in the middle of a business district. There were no other houses on our street, just an array of businesses. There was an Asian food mart next door and a local poker bar on the north corner. On the south corner stood a landmark restaurant called The Hayward Ranch. Across the street, a flourishing car dealership covered most of the block. On a daily basis, I would see car salesmen coercing potential buyers to purchase used vehicles. Our new neighbors were drastically different than the typical neighbors you could bother for a cup of sugar. Shortly after our move to Hayward, my youngest brother Terrance became the newest addition to our family. With five children, my mother, and Terrance's father, we had a full house. But our family was nothing like the family on the hit

ABC television series *Full House*. We were Black, broke, and bereaved from the happiness displayed in those entertaining episodes. My mother was showing signs of fatigue and post-natal stress. Terrance was a needy infant, Lanette was a blossoming young girl, and I was a mischievous little kid. My older brothers were growing into men and didn't get along with Terrance's father. However, he didn't stay around long enough to watch the season change, so I didn't have time to form my own opinion about him.

MY FIRST HOME IN HAYWARD, CALIFORNIA

When Terrance's father departed, my mother was left to raise all her children on her own. That's when I noticed, even at the tender age of seven, that our family was beginning to break down. Though experienced with computers, my mother wasn't working. She was content with government funding being our only reliable source of income. And those government checks didn't last long either since my mother had an escalating crack cocaine habit. Every first and fifteenth of the month when my mother got paid, a combination of drug dealers and drug addicts were familiar guests at our home. The drug dealers eagerly anticipated the amount of federal currency that would end up in their pockets. Some dealers even accepted food stamps as payment for drugs. This was a growing epidemic across the United States, especially in the Black community. My mother was no different, a powerless slave for the next hit. She started looking high on crack cocaine more often. She would pace around the house *cleaning*, which meant picking up anything small and white on the carpet. Crack addicts often mistake anything that is small and white for crack cocaine. The skin on her fingertips looked chapped and dry from being burned from the crack pipe. And she would pick at the skin with her fingernails, which was always a pet peeve on mine. When she spoke, her mouth would take the form of a devilish smirk and her words had a trembling tone. Her clothes had a stench of crack cocaine smoke. She was a disappointing representation of the strong Black woman.

Even though things around me were progressively getting worse, my behavior remained the same. Though far from an angel, I wasn't a bad kid considering the trouble I could have gotten myself into at nine years old. I lied, but wasn't a liar. I got into fights, but wasn't a trouble maker. I stole, but wasn't a thief. Okay, maybe once or twice I fit the mold of a thief. The owners of the Asian mart next door would find out firsthand how much like a thief I could be. Every day I would go to Burbank Elementary and see other students at lunchtime buying chips and ice cream with money given to them by their parents. Free lunch students like me didn't have the luxury of purchasing those items, so I had to find a way to get some money on my own. One morning before going to school, I decided that I was going to break into the neighboring Asian mart. Days prior to that morning, I noticed store workers on the rooftop of the Asian mart next door. I watched as they disappeared through a door located on the roof. The door was similar to an attic door in a house, which allowed access in and out of the store through the roof. My master plan was to climb up to the roof, open that door, and enter the store. I knew precisely the layout of the store, since my mother often sent me there to purchase random grocery items. Back in the day, Black kids happily went to the store for their mother, even to purchase cigarettes or beer. My mother would often send me to the store to buy Newport menthols with a hand written note explaining whom the purchase was for. So I went outside, climbed a fence that scaled the store wall, and pulled myself up on top of the roof. Once I was up there, I acknowledged that someone could possibly see me from the street, so I lowered my body and walked in a duck-like motion. When I reached the door, I pulled up on the door handle, and to my surprise, it was unlocked. I noticed a small ladder attached to the door, which lowered down into the store. I climbed down the ladder, which put me right in the middle of the same store I had been to so many times as a customer. As soon as my feet hit the floor I scanned the room. My heart immediately began beating hard and fast. It felt as if my heart was pounding, like King Kong pounds on his chest in the movies. At that moment, I realized that I had actually committed a crime. I had reached the point of no return. If I was caught breaking into this store, either I was going to jail or getting my ass beat by my mother. Both of which were equally as bad because my mother didn't only spank us with her hand, she also used a telephone extension cord. The cord hurt like hell, and left welts on my body afterwards as a lasting reminder of the ass whooping I had just received. Back then, spanking your child with more than your hand wasn't considered child abuse. It was just a good old-fashioned ass-whooping from your parent.

Initially, I didn't know what I wanted to steal. All the snacks I'd wanted to buy from this store in the past, but couldn't afford it, were now there for the taking. Even though the majority of their items were labeled in a foreign language, it didn't fool me. I knew bubble gum when I saw it. After taking visual inventory of all the chips and candy in the store, my attention quickly shifted to the cash register. I hoped the register contained money. If it did, the money could buy all the snacks my little heart desired. I walked over to the cash register, which for some reason was already opened, and saw nothing but coins inside. To a true burglar, the sight of nothing but dimes, nickels, and quarters would be a disappointment. But to a third grader, this was a jackpot. I snatched all the coins my little hands could hold and stuffed them into my stonewashed jean pockets. I did this until there was only about seven or eight coins left in each slot. I hoped that at first glance, the store workers wouldn't notice that the money was missing. With my pockets full and jingling with coins, I retreated out of the store the same way I had entered. Once back on the ground, I scurried off to school in pure joy. That day, I bought at least two or three ice creams during the lunch period. I was balling out of control for a third grader.

My temporary financial gain didn't solve my problems at home. My family was falling apart rapidly, one person at a time. My brother Derell wasted no time moving out to stay with friends, disgusted by the drug-addicted woman my mother had become. At sixteen years old, he had already seen enough. Besides, Derell had to focus on his promising basketball career. Eugene Jr., an aspiring rap star and local drug dealer, used our residence as a pit stop. Maybe it was too hard to sell drugs out of the same house where someone else was using them. Sadly, it wouldn't be long before Eugene was arrested, convicted, and sent to a juvenile detention center in Santa Cruz, CA. Shortly thereafter, my sister moved out of the house as well. She left to live with her friend who also lived in Hayward, and went to the same high school. Lanette's move left Terrance and I as the only two stranded in the household to witness our mother's self-destruction.

Over time, Terrance and I experienced so much turmoil and pain together. We were always at risk, yet hardly watched over or protected because my mother was constantly high. We began to change residences frequently too. We moved from apartment to apartment, including living in the homes of people my mother could have known for a long time, or could have just met that week. As children, you don't have any control over what your parents do. You follow your parent's guidance believing that they have your best interest at heart. It was in these homes that my attitude changed for the worst and my internal rage grew. I absolutely hated living in other people's homes. The lack of ownership of a small toy or personal space made me not want to be anyone's houseguest. I didn't have a bicycle, bedroom, or even a bed to claim as my own. I remember once while staying in the home of my mother's friend, Terrance was infected with the chicken pox. Since most people become immune to chicken pox after being infected once, my mother thought it would be a great idea to kill two birds with one stone. She forced me to be in the presence of my younger brother while he was infected with chicken pox, so that I could be infected as well at the same time. She thought this was a brilliant idea, while applying calamine lotion to my sores for the next week made me miserable. I now have a physical scar on the left side of my neck as a reminder of those dreadful chicken pox. These childhood experiences even affected my teenage years. When my peers got their first car from their parents, I felt cheated because I didn't have that same financial support from my parents.

From other people's homes, we moved to homeless shelters. If you are not familiar with homeless shelters, they're usually run by non-profit organizations such as The Salvation Army or Red Cross. They are usually overcrowded with families of battered women and drug rehabbers. Although these homeless shelters appeared spacious — with their drab gray walls, waiting room furniture, and army barrack style dormitories, there was little personal privacy or space. We shared community bathrooms and ate meals in cafeteria style dining halls. Each resident had to leave the shelter at a certain time in the morning and return before a set time in the evening or be locked out. The purpose of this rule was to encourage its occupants to seek work or permanent residence elsewhere, rather than becoming complacent and comfortable at the shelter. Often our possessions would be stolen by the time we returned home, which really bothered me because I didn't have much to lose to begin with. We were repeatedly robbed of common toiletries like toothpaste and soap. And we tried our luck every time we placed an item in the community refrigerator. Nothing was safe in this communal living space.

Terrance and I spent most of our time playing video games on our Nintendo gaming system we hooked up to the small television near our bedside. Though I disliked the shelter life, I managed to find solace in my situation because I was still in the presence of family. We loved our mother because she was ours, which made her special to us, even though she was not perfect. She was still the one we both looked to for love and guidance. As the late Tupac Shakur once stated in a song, *"even as a crack fiend mama—she always was a Black queen mama."*

Surprisingly, shelter life didn't last long because my mother found an apartment in downtown Hayward. The lower level, two-bedroom apartment was positioned near the entrance of the Palomar Terrace Apartments. Our return to Hayward was pleasant for quite some time. I attended elementary school at Park Elementary, while Terrance was enrolled in a nearby preschool. My mother appeared to be getting back on her feet and showing signs of progress. Although her drug problem was still apparent, it did not seem to consume her life as it once did. But it would not be long before drugs caused our living situation to take a turn for the worse.

One late night, while I was sleeping in my room, I heard my mother frantically screaming from her bedroom. I jumped out of bed, and sprinted down the hallway to my mother's bedroom. The door was closed shut, but unlocked. I barged into the bedroom to find my mother in the strong grasp of some strange half naked man. Within seconds, I retreated from the bedroom, darted to the kitchen, and grabbed a butcher's knife out of the drawer. With the knife in hand and my heart racing, I returned to the room with the sole intention of stabbing this stranger to death. Once I entered the room, the man immediately noticed the knife I was holding. His eyes bulged even larger than they already were, going from baseball size to softball size. In an instant, he turned and leaped out of an opened first floor bedroom window and disappeared into the night. After glaring at my mother in shock mixed with disgust, I dropped my head only to see a makeshift crack pipe made out of a ballpoint pen and aluminum foil. They had been getting high together on crack, and for whatever reason, the situation got out of hand.

It would not be the last time my mother's safety was jeopardized over drugs. She was often beaten by dope dealers because she owed them money or by fellow addicts because they wanted to smoke up all of her crack. Many times as a young boy, I would try to fight the pushers myself. I was angered that they were feeding my mother this poison. Though I was not much of a threat to these grown adults, I tried my hardest to fight them off. I could have been seriously injured or hurt by one of these criminals. What bothered me even more than feeling powerless against stopping the destruction of mother, was inhaling the sickening smell of burning crack cocaine. My mom often smoked in the bathroom or in her bedroom with the door shut. Therefore, the suffocating smell would seep from underneath the door into the open air. Based on the scent alone, I knew when my mother was getting high. It was a familiar, distinct smell that I will never forget.

I needed a way out, a quick escape route from all the madness. Since I couldn't just pack up and leave, I found peace and comfort in the public school system. Contrary to what most people might think, I loved being at school despite my living situation. For those eight hours, I could lose myself in classroom activities and recess. I could be around friends and forget everything else that was going on in my life. Simply, just enjoy being a kid. Knowing that the life waiting for me after school was unpleasant, pushed me to be a good student and get good grades. I tried to behave at school to avoid being suspended and sent home. Despite my school suspension records, I sincerely never wanted to be disobedient, it just happened at times. It's amazing that I was ever able to function at school, knowing that I had no stable home to return to after school.

At about the age of ten, we changed addresses again. Due to the change, I switched schools again and began attending Cherryland Elementary School. As a fifth-grader at Cherryland, I met a friend named Alex. Since we shared several of the same interests, Alex and I spent a lot of time together at school. We both enjoyed the competitive playground games of flag football, basketball and tetherball. We both also loved music and dancing. In fact, our love for dancing led to the creation of our school dance group. Our crew mimicked Another Bad Creation, a popular U.S. preteen boy band at the time. Our dance group had swag with our airbrushed overalls (one strap down), rayon shirts, and Gumbi-style haircuts. I was always donned in overalls with the infamous Bart Simpson painted on one leg and my childhood nickname "Chewy" on the other. Alex and I had a special friendship, inseparable at times. I would spend hours at his house, either inside playing video games or outside getting dirty and sweaty playing any game that included a ball.

MY CREW INCLUDING MY BROTHER ALEX (FAR LEFT)

Alex had what I considered a *normal* home, because he had both his mother and father living under the same roof. Alex also had two younger siblings; a brother named Donovan and a sister named Shalawn. They were the model middle class family of five. Every time I visited their home, I didn't want to leave. Eventually, I mustered up the courage to ask if I could move in with Alex. They had what I always desired in a home, and I could not wait to be part of it. I wanted to have my own bed, a closet to hang my clothes, and a dresser to place my socks and underwear. It may seem simple to most, but I desired what most kids take for granted every day. My mom and Alex's parents both agreed to let me move in, making me the next child to leave my mother's side at age eleven.

Unfortunately, my brother was left as the only one still under my mother's unreliable supervision. When my older brothers left, my sister was still around for guidance. When my sister left, Terrance and I leaned on each other. But when I left, my five-year-old brother had it bad all by himself. He was continuously left alone in public at the tender age of five. My mom would take him to places like Chuck E. Cheese and leave him stranded there alone. Sadly, my mother made a place where a kid was supposed to feel happy, utterly terrifying for Terrance. In my opinion, being abandoned by my mother at an early age continued to affect Terrance as an adult. He would never stop seeking the love and affection that he never received from my mother as a child.

My mother's repeated action of leaving Terrance at random, eventually landed my brother in foster care. He would remain in the foster care system until my mother took a break from getting high and sought to regain custody of her child. I was already familiar with the foster care system, being sporadically placed in foster homes myself. However, the reasons why I became custody of the state were different from my brother's. I was in foster care because at times my mother couldn't control me, so she would voluntarily surrender custody. For example, one sunny afternoon, I decided to steal money from my mother's purse just hours after she cashed her government check. With a wad of money in my pocket, I went to Bayfair Mall on a shopping spree. After purchasing about three bags full of clothing and shoes, I bought myself a sleeping bag from Woolworth. I didn't know where I was going to sleep—maybe in the neighborhood tree house. But I definitely couldn't return home after what I just did. With bags in hand, I headed to the arcade to play video games. Back then, kids didn't have high-tech gaming systems at their leisure, so arcade games were extremely popular. I spent quarter after quarter, playing games like Street Fighter and Shinobi well into the dark of the night. I was utterly afraid of the streets at night, so when the mall closed, roaming Hayward after dark was frightening. Therefore, I called the police myself and let them know where I was located and the situation I was in. Minutes later, I was in a police car on my way to the Hayward Police Station. These actions led to one of my many placements in foster care.

Though set up for good reasons, foster care was never pleasant to me. Many foster parents already have kids of their own, whom hate to share their space and their toys with a new stranger in the house. As a foster child, I always felt there was an invisible divider that kept me from uniting with my new family.

There was nothing in the home that led me to believe that I was a part of the family, I was just leasing a family for a limited time only. Quite frankly, the children in the homes would let me know that I didn't belong, which ignited my anger. In my rage, I would start fights with the other children or break their toys. I even tried running away from a couple of foster homes because I desperately wanted to be back with my biological family, for better or worse. But living with Alex felt different. His family opened their home to me and allowed me to have fun and enjoy being a child. Furthermore, the kids in the house viewed me as their older brother, which was very welcoming. I now had strong family support, and a stable home to call my own. My life was starting to accumulate many joyful experiences that I could cherish for a lifetime.

2ND INNING:

While living with Alex, I began to fall in love with the game of baseball. Although I was no stranger to the game, I never wanted to play baseball as much as I did while living with my new brother. Baseball was always fun with Alex, no matter how we played it. Sometimes we played inside the house, using a sofa pillow as a baseball bat and a pair of rolled up tube socks for a baseball. Other times we played baseball outside by fiercely competing in a game called "strikeout." Unlike people on the East Coast with their love for "stickball," our neighborhood favorite on the West Side was strikeout. All we needed was a bat (wooden or metal), a tennis ball (sometimes two or three balls if the other's got lost), and something to draw a strike zone on the wall (often tree bark or crayon). With two or more people, we played multiple innings of exciting baseball. Balls and strikes were determined by the strike zone drawn on the wall. The strike zone was a box about three feet wide, and shin to waist high. If a ball was pitched inside the box, it was a strike. If pitched outside the box, it was a ball. On a batted ball, if the defender caught the ball in the air or on one bounce, then it was an out. The defense had to get three outs before switching sides. Singles, doubles, triples, and home runs were decided by how far you hit the ball. Since we often played outside of our apartment complex, a home run would be a ball hit past the car parked across the street. This is how I learned the game of baseball. For years, I begged my mom to sign me up for baseball tryouts at the local Little League with no success. My mother could not envision sacrificing $40 for me to play Little League baseball when she could use that money to buy crack. On the other hand, Alex played baseball for Hayward West National Little League. Therefore, signing me up for organized baseball was a simple process for my new parents.

They made sure I was registered to participate in the upcoming baseball season. It wasn't until I got older that I noticed the progressive drop of Black kids participating in Little League baseball. Participation decreased dramatically at the Little League level, which created a domino effect of participation shortage in all of baseball. Less Black kids playing Little League baseball naturally resulted in less high school baseball players. Less Black high school baseball players, created a limited amount of kids to recruit for collegiate baseball. Therefore, there were less Black college players with the opportunity to play professional baseball. By process of elimination, there were less Black Minor League baseball players lucky enough to make it to the Major Leagues. This nasty cycle repeats itself because Black kids no longer have Black superstar players to emulate, thus creating an overall lack of interest in baseball. As a Black kid growing up in the 90's, I could relate to Ken Griffey Jr. I could see myself as a Major League Baseball superstar, because Griffey Jr. looked just like me. It was totally different watching Mark McGwire at the Oakland Coliseum, than it was watching Ken Griffey Jr. I believe that in order to regain the interest of Black kids in baseball, this entire cycle must be broken.

Hayward West National baseball tryouts were held at Burbank Elementary school. When I arrived at tryouts, the first thing I noticed was all the baseball equipment on the field. There were baseball pitching machines, shiny metal bats, and glossy new batting helmets. I remember thinking how cool the equipment looked since I never needed all this stuff to play strikeout. During tryouts, the kids were full of energy. They were running around impatiently waiting their turn to showcase their talent. All the moms were helping their kids prepare for tryouts by putting on their cleats, or making last-minute adjustments to their baseball pants. Dads scanned the field from behind the fence, nervously hoping all the days of playing catch in the park with their sons would pay off. We went through tryouts in groups, all getting the chance to hit, run and throw. When it was my turn to hit, I felt an immense pressure to perform while everyone was watching. I wanted to do so well that everyone would praise me afterwards for my batting skills. I would never relinquish that feeling I had that morning while hitting. The feeling of nervous anxiety is something competitive athletes have to control throughout their career. For a twelve year old, experiencing baseball tryouts for the first time, I did just fine.

I batted a few balls with satisfaction, but even back then, I had passion for hitting the long ball.

There were eight teams in the league, some of which I quickly found out were more appealing than others because of their winning history. My performance at tryouts that day landed me on Rich's Tigers baseball team. The Tigers were infamous for being a bad baseball team, similar to the Bad News Bears. But since organized baseball was all new to me, Rich's Tigers historical losing record didn't matter much to me. Hayward West National league games began the weekend following tryouts. I was excited to be a part of a real baseball team and couldn't wait to begin playing games.

MY FIRST BASEBALL TEAM, RICH'S TIGERS OF HAYWARD WEST NATIONAL

Opening day commenced with a parade for the league. All the teams lined the field with their players in uniform. Each coach and player was announced, and photos were taken. The first game started at the conclusion of opening day ceremonies. From the first game, I struggled playing organized baseball. I never before interacted with umpires or played baseball with so many rules. Whenever rules were inconsistently enforced, I believed every umpire was a cheater. If I struck out on a called strike by the umpire, I would throw my bat or helmet in disagreement and disgust. And while headed back to the dugout, my head would be down as I dragged my feet the entire way. Bad sportsmanship was no stranger to kids where I'm from. In fact, it was extremely common and accepted by most coaches and parents. We didn't have many fathers around to teach us how to play with integrity and deal with failure. Therefore, if we won, I felt great. But if we lost, it was as if the world had just ended.

Accepting both my successes and failures continued to be a learning lesson for me with every game. I wasn't like the other kids who had played tee ball at five years old and continued to play each year thereafter. They had an early jump on learning both the mechanics of baseball and how to deal with their emotions. As for me, I was just getting my feet wet at age twelve. That was no excuse for behaving in such a manner, and the league let me know that they wouldn't stand for it. If I wanted to play baseball, I would have to abide by the Little League code of conduct. My desire to play baseball, kept my behavior in check, well...for the most part. Just like any twelve year old kid, sometimes I just could not control my emotions.

Another place where I enjoyed the game of baseball was at the Boys & Girls Club of Hayward. The club offered a safe and fun environment for youth to spend time, at a low membership price. I went to the club daily, staying until it closed its doors at night. While inside, I played all types of exciting table games like bumper pool and foosball. I also made model cars, weaved lanyards, and even ran 1,000 laps around the gymnasium to win a trip to a nearby water park. There was so much stuff I could do there to stay off the streets and out of trouble. While other kids were subjecting themselves to a life in the streets, I took refuge at the Boys & Girls Club. The instructors genuinely cared about each and every one of us. They disciplined us by suspension from the club if we acted inappropriately, which taught me to take responsibility for my actions. For a kid that wants to be at the club every day, being suspended was capital punishment. Looking back on it, going to the Boys & Girls Club was one of the most beneficial things that happened in my life because it helped me become a better person. It also helped me become a better baseball player.

Almost every chance I got, I participated in whiffle baseball games at the club. The game was intriguing because of how difficult it was to hit a whiffle ball square. Hitting a whiffle ball requires good hand and eye coordination, because the ball moves unexpectedly when pitched. Because a whiffle ball has multiple holes in its plastic surface, and a hollowed core, it moves unpredictably once it's in the air. We played numerous whiffle ball games and tournaments inside the gymnasium. The games were fun and easy to play since minimal equipment was required. We only needed a whiffle ball and a plastic bat, since you can catch the ball with your hand. Hitting whiffle balls at the Boys & Girls Club improved my batting skills. If I could hit a whiffle ball when it's pitched, then I could definitely hit a Little League baseball.

Once I reached age fourteen, I started believing I was good at baseball. I had already been selected to a couple of Little League all-star teams, despite only playing organized baseball for two years. Quickly, I gained a reputation on the field for hitting home runs and having terrorizing speed on the bases. Coaches from several select baseball teams began inviting me to travel with them to play in tournaments at no cost. Without their generosity, I would have never been able to afford to pay for the cost of playing travel baseball. Thankfully, I was blessed to play for free while other players paid costly registration fees and traveling expenses. It was beneficial to interact with kids from different areas because it exposed me to various lifestyles and cultures. It also allowed me to learn different styles of playing baseball. I made a lot of friends over the years from the teams I played on. At this juncture of my life, baseball was good, and life was good.

But after a few years of living with Alex, I began to feel as if I had worn out my welcome in their home. Though his family had always treated me as if I was one of their own, I think I was garnering too much attention. Just like the addition of a newborn baby to a family already with kids, my presence created some natural jealousy from my new siblings towards me. Instead of being treated like an asset to the family, they started acting like I was disrupting the family unity. Maybe it was the shortage of space, with three growing boys and a young girl in a small apartment. Or maybe it was the weekly food consumption that can hit a parent hard in their bank account. Besides, I was a growing teenager whose needs were increasing every day. Or maybe it was just me over-analyzing the situation, and feeling like I was a burden on the family.

Whatever the case, after completing the eighth grade, I asked my brother Derell if I could move in with him. Derell had recently become a new father to his first child, a baby boy named Jalen. Living in a one-bedroom apartment with the mother of his child and my nephew, Derell knew he didn't have ample space for me stay there comfortably. But despite the living conditions, Derell agreed to let me move in with them. I changed homes once again. The move caused some tension to seep into the relationship between Alex and myself. Alex mistakenly believed that by moving out, I had wronged his family for all they had done. I never intended to offend his family in any way. I just wanted to reconnect with my biological family. It wasn't the last time Alex felt disrespected by the personal life decisions I've made. Regardless of how he felt, I had to make the best decision for my life.

At the Jimerson residence, I didn't have a bedroom or a bed to myself. I merely had a pillow and a blanket to make a pallet on the floor to sleep on. In the morning, I would fold my blanket and place it in the hallway closet along with my pillow. If I was hungry, I had to make my own meal and clean up after myself in the kitchen. At fourteen years old, I knew that I had to be proactive about taking care of myself while living with my brother. But I was okay with that because I had already created this mindset of being self-sufficient. At least now I had another opportunity to live amongst family.

After moving in with Derell in the summer of 1994, I used my break from school to help out around the house. I helped Derell with the household chores and babysitting my nephew. It was my first experience taking care of a young child other than the few times I looked after Terrance. I remember using Johnson & Johnson baby wash to bathe Jalen, and a plastic Taco Bell cup of water to rinse him off. It was pleasing to nurture and care for a young boy in ways that I never experienced as a toddler. In the fall of 1994, I began my high school years attending Hayward High School. Every morning, I rode the AC Transit public transportation bus to the Hayward hills in the mornings to get to school. As a freshman at Hayward High, I played three sports on the junior varsity squads: baseball, basketball and football. It was my first experience socializing with high school students and teammates. Although, I enjoyed Hayward High for the most part, I never felt completely comfortable on campus. The school was home to the rich kids, and I was light years away from rich. Students there had to have the finest clothes and be hip to the latest fashion trends to be respected as a person. I couldn't possibly compete, because I was just trying to put together some decent cheap outfits to wear to school. My household tax bracket didn't match up with all the other students who came from a family with money.

I also never completely felt comfortable living with Derell. As a growing teenage boy, my needs and desires didn't match up with my brother's requests and demands. He was focused on himself, while I needed him to care for me and teach me how to become a man. For example, Derell purchased a new Nissan Sentra while I was living with him. The money he used to buy the car was money from a trust fund in my name. Since my father experienced a serious back injury on the job, a portion of his settlement payout was delegated to me in a trust fund. My father and Derell agreed to use the trust fund to help purchase a family car, and cover my living expenses. Instead, Derell used this money to buy himself a personal vehicle, and not family vehicle. It was never used to transport me to, or from school. And despite having my driver's permit, I was never allowed to drive the vehicle. Maybe he suffered from something I would later struggle with myself: a natural uncontrollable selfish attitude. I believe it results from being deprived of material items growing up as a child. Once these items are attained later in life, the deprived person selfishly guards over their possessions. Following my freshman school year, I decided I didn't want to stay with my brother anymore. My sister, with whom I had always remained close with throughout all the bouncing around, had just gotten her own two-bedroom apartment near Hayward High School. In the past, Lanette would constantly express her intention to get both Terrance and I under her care. Now that she had her own home supported by her twenty year old income, the time had arrived. I abruptly left Derell's home to go live with my sister. I didn't realize until I became a man myself, how much living with Derell influenced my life. The way he dressed, the Polo Sport brand cologne he wore, and how clean he kept his home are just a few examples of how he shaped my adult life. Although we continued to have a brotherly relationship over the years, the days of living with Derell formed an emotional wedge between us. Spending time living with him revealed some traits of his that I did not like. Therefore, I guarded myself from being emotionally hurt by him in the future, by distancing myself away from him.

Living with my sister was dramatically different than my stay with Derell. Born in August, with her dominant personality, there is no doubt that Lanette's zodiac sign is a Leo. She always believed she could do things better than the next person. And she definitely believed that she could take better care of her younger brothers than anyone else could, even better than our own mother. Months after I moved into Lanette's home, she also gained custody of our younger brother Terrance. It was now the three of us collectively depending on each other for love, support, and care.

LANETTE'S TWO-BEDROOM APARTMENT IN HAYWARD, CALIFORNIA

3RD INNING:

Though my move to Lanette's house placed me geographically closer to Hayward High, I decided to transfer high schools my sophomore year. I handed in my pitchfork as a Hayward Farmer, to become a Mount Eden Monarch. Mt. Eden High School was the cross-town rival of Hayward High. Living with Lanette placed me right the backyard of my enemies. Though I didn't understand the magnitude of my decision to change high schools at the time, I now realize that changing schools was one of the best decisions I ever made. Unlike Hayward High, I could be myself at Mt. Eden. I could go to school with whatever clothes I had in my closet and not be teased because of what I had on. I didn't need to wear the latest Jordans to be accepted. All I needed to do was go to school and be myself. The student body at Mt. Eden respected those who stayed true to themselves. Plus all my old friends and former classmates from Winton Junior High attended Mt. Eden as well. I rode two AC Transit public transportation buses from my house on "D" Street to school every day. I caught Line 95 to Hayward Bart, and then transferred to Line 86 all the way to Mt. Eden. Day after day, I saw the same kids on the same buses. Some kids attended Mt. Eden as well, while some were traveling to other public schools. Every day I would meet my close friend Eric Handy, who also traveled the long distance on the bus to Mt. Eden. Not many students had cars, so riding AC Transit buses were common means of transportation to school.

I felt comfortable being at Mt. Eden, and I was extremely comfortable living in my sister's home. My sister always had a naturally caring and giving spirit. Maybe it was because of her position as the middle child in the family.

Or maybe because she was the only girl, sandwiched between four boys. But something about her nurturing personality made me feel like everything was gonna be all right while living under her roof. In Lanette's home, Terrance and I shared a bedroom with side-by-side twin beds, a common dresser, and a closet big enough to stuff with our clothes and junk.

With a solid family base at home, competing in team sports at Mt. Eden didn't seem as mentally and physically challenging. I continued to play all three sports at Mt. Eden during my sophomore year, just as I did at Hayward High. But my athletic career as a Monarch began a little differently, starting with junior varsity football. Due to my athleticism, it seemed like I was placed on the football field almost every play of the season. I primarily played wide receiver on offense and defensive back on defense. I was also on the kick return, punt return, kickoff, and field goal units. Believe me, like Randy Moss striding down the sideline, all I wanted to do was catch touchdown passes. I had no desire to tackle muscle-necked running backs! For that exact reason, I would never play high school football again. Football, proved to be too macho for my liking. At fifteen years old, risking my health for a high school football team that wasn't very good seemed foolish. And I definitely didn't want to keep doing football drills until my heart felt like it was going to explode.

Once basketball season arrived, being a Mt. Eden Monarch became extremely fun. Not only did I enjoy the transition from one sport to the next, but I also enjoyed the buzz that filled the campus during basketball season. The highly respected Mt. Eden varsity basketball team was holding tryouts. The notorious Ron Benevides headed the varsity squad, while his pupils managed the junior varsity and freshman teams. Benevides was known as the high school version of Bobby Knight. His disciplinarian style and in-game yelling and screaming fits only added strands to his already gray hair. Benevides not only made a name for the Mt. Eden basketball team, but he also selfishly aimed to make a name for himself.

To my surprise, I made the varsity squad as a sophomore. Joining the Mt. Eden varsity basketball team as a sophomore was a huge accomplishment. The team was comprised of all types of players from different ethnic backgrounds. We had an unbelievable Mexican point guard named Jorge Salaiz, combined with talented Black forwards Jawahsa Carter and Stephen Walker. Though excited to be on the team, I wasn't prepared to deal with a man who would continually test my character and mental strength. Benevides repeatedly berated his players during games in front of the fans for the slightest mental or physical mistake. Benevides was a monster on the basketball court, and I was fed up with his antics. Because of his coaching style, I could not wait for the season to be over. Unfortunately, Benevides was also the varsity baseball coach, taking his basketball ways to the baseball field. Despite my dislike for Benevides, I decided to play varsity baseball that year. He was even worst as a baseball coach. One game, our shortstop made an error in the first inning. Upset about the fielding error, Benevides took the player out of the game in the first inning. Didn't he know that once you're out of a baseball game, you can't be substituted back into the game? This was not basketball! His coaching technique was wearing me out. I had already put up with the madness during basketball season. I couldn't handle the same during the baseball season. Although I wanted to quit, my love for the game of baseball powered me through the bullshit. I also believed in the notion that once you quit something for the first time, you always will have the propensity to quit anything.

After completing my sophomore year at Mt. Eden, I returned in 1996 for my junior year. I was looking forward to playing another exciting season of high school basketball. Being a member of the Mt. Eden varsity basketball team was like playing for the Harlem Globetrotters. Similar to the Harlem Globetrotters, each player was privileged to don the infamous blue and gold striped warm ups. We also got to travel like them too. We participated in basketball tournaments in both Redding and Arcata, California. But the highlight of our basketball tour, was playing in Ketchikan, Alaska. The Clark Cochrane Christmas Classic is an annual high school basketball tournament held in Ketchikan, Alaska. The tournament welcomes basketball teams from all over the United States, Canada, and Australia. Ketchikan, Alaska, also known as "The Salmon Capitol of the World," is the southernmost city in Alaska. Around 1996, the demographics of Hayward, California and Ketchikan, Alaska were polar opposites. With less than 1% total Black population in Ketchikan, our basketball team of mostly Black players was something that the city was not accustomed to. While in Alaska, the players on our team lived in the homes of host families. Most of these families had students who attended the high school hosting the tournament. The parents volunteered to open their home to us for the duration of the tournament. Many of the students housing players were females. So when we weren't playing basketball in the tournament, we were socializing with the female hosts and their friends. The girls in Alaska were not shy about revealing their hidden attraction for Black males. The players on my team took full advantage of being viewed as *different* or *exotic* by the women of Ketchikan. For the few days we were there, we ran the show on the basketball court, and ran circles around the girls off the court. Ironically, I spent my time in Alaska hanging out with a white girl name Pepper. Who would have ever thought that white girls from Alaska were attracted to Black guys from the 'hood. We literally felt like NBA superstars for about a week. High school basketball had never before been more entertaining.

After basketball season ended, I refused to play another season of baseball for Benevides. His coaching style—compared to how the game of baseball is supposed to be played—did not match up. I opted not to play high school baseball for the first time in my life, all because of Benevides. It was extremely difficult to take a break from playing a sport during the school year. I was not accustomed to all the free time the majority of students on campus had the liberty to enjoy. There were no practices, games, or extracurricular activities to attend. This period should have been more enjoyable, yet I missed being on the baseball field every day. It's funny because whenever I was playing a baseball season, I wished for days off and free time. But when I was away from the game, I missed it daily and couldn't wait to get back on the field. Besides, too much free time as a high school student only meant more time for me to possibly get in trouble. Though not playing baseball for Mt. Eden, I continued to play baseball during the summer months. I traveled with a Connie Mack league team, playing baseball throughout Northern California and Nevada.

Once my senior year arrived, I knew it was my last chance to play baseball at Mt. Eden. In 1997, I continued to play basketball as I had in previous years. Surprisingly, over the three years at Mt. Eden, I had become a high school basketball star. At shooting guard, I averaged thirteen points a game to propel our basketball team to an East Bay top 25 ranking. We remained ranked all season long and stormed through the Hayward Area Athletic League (HAAL) play-offs. We went on to win the Northern California Section (NCS) championship on a last second shot by teammate Doug Lymon. We eventually lost in the first round of the state playoffs to Vacaville High School. The players on that 1997 team orchestrated one of the best basketball seasons in school history. The bond of friendship I built with guys like Darrell Taylor, Armond Wainright, and Alfred Dyer would thrive long after high school ended.

With no buzz over my basketball skills from college recruiters, I switched my focus to the baseball field. There was a different leader on the diamond this year. Coach Ted Muniz replaced Benevides as the head varsity baseball coach at Mt. Eden. Ted Muniz (also known as Officer Ted Muniz) was also a gang unit police officer for the City of Hayward. Gang activity was growing in Hayward back then. There were a slew of gangs in the area, like the "A" Street Nortenos and DGF. Many students at Mt. Eden fell right into the allure of gang life. Coach Muniz' connection with the local youth through his police work made him more reputable with his players, and we respected him for that. With a new coach managing the team, I felt more comfortable putting on a Mt. Eden baseball jersey.

With school funding scarce and no extra help from outside sponsors, Coach Muniz did his best to prepare the team to compete in the HAAL. Unlike our basketball team, we didn't have a winning reputation in baseball, so our financial support was minimal. It's funny how folks only financially support winning programs, instead of investing in the youth of America. There were potholes in the outfield grass, limited dirt in some areas of the infield, and no outfield fence. For a home run, we simply hit the ball as far as we could and ran. For practices, Coach Muniz would drive his patrol car to school and park near the baseball field. Each day his car was at risk of being hit by an errant thrown baseball. And he could care less about his car being damaged. The most important thing for Coach Muniz was teaching his players life lessons through baseball. I was excited about my senior season of baseball at Mt. Eden and looked forward to playing for Coach Muniz.

Although I was a pretty good baseball player, most of my peers did not realize that I played baseball at Mt. Eden. Generally speaking, people only mentioned my name when talking basketball at Mt. Eden. All my friends were my basketball teammates, so naturally I was commonly associated with the "Hoop Squad." The Hoop Squad was my crew at Mt. Eden. We were a band of brothers who loved the game of basketball, and had each other's back. Since most of us didn't have fathers around, our bond was bigger than basketball. The Hoop Squad was like family to us. We were well known in the city of Hayward for stealing the show on and off the basketball court. Since I was in-season playing baseball, I kept myself occupied while my friends were constantly flirting with trouble. However, sometimes, the trouble was just too enticing for me to avoid. One day, I received word that my friend Armond was hospitalized with a head wound. A student from rival Hayward High School hit Armond in the back of the head with a glass bottle. Since our group of basketball players were a tight knit group, if you messed with one of us, you messed with all of us. Therefore, the next day we jumped in our vehicles and drove across town to Hayward High School looking for the student who did this. Our group of about fifteen members from the Hoop Squad marched across campus at Hayward High during lunch. Students could tell that we were not there to play basketball, but instead there to fight. Unfortunately, the dude we were looking for got word of our arrival and left school before we could find him. Therefore, we decided to beat up anyone who looked at us the wrong way. A few students from Hayward High got knocked out that afternoon in retaliation for what happened to Armond. The next day, the word got back to campus at Mt. Eden. I was called into the principal's office and subsequently suspended for my role in the campus brawl. My suspension put a black mark on the great season I was having on the baseball field. At that moment, I knew that in order to remain focused on playing baseball, I needed to distance myself from my friends. In life, sometimes you have to step away from the social scene to prevent being distracted from reaching your goals.

When I returned to playing baseball at Mt. Eden, I began to make a name for myself in baseball. The word around town started to get out that I was a gifted baseball player. My batting average and slugging percentage increased dramatically. My stolen bases were among top of the league, and my athletic ability on the baseball field was second-to-none. Due to my performance, I was named co-Prep of the Week by the Daily Review, the local area newspaper.

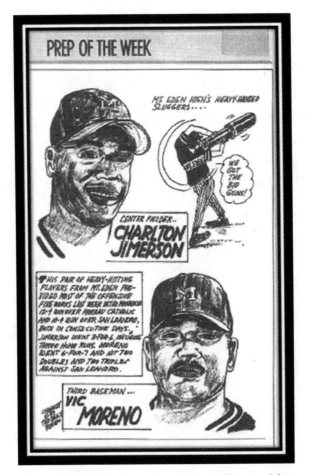

BASH BROTHERS: CHARLTON JIMERSON & VICTOR MORENO

I played extremely well my senior year, hitting .424 with four home runs (three at home without a fence) for the season. My performance caught the attention of local Houston Astros scout, Gene Wellman. Founder of Wellman Batting Cages in Hayward, Mr. Wellman was a prominent baseball figure in Hayward. After watching me play and gathering more information about my tools, Mr. Wellman sent my personal information to Houston. He expressed to the Astros front office his desire to draft me in the 1997 Major League Baseball Amateur Draft. They concurred and I was selected by the Houston Astros in the 24th round (760th overall) as a "draft-and-follow" pick. Draft-and-follow is a common term and procedure in baseball that means an organization has drafted a player that they plan to follow in the future. It usually results in a player going to college to continue playing baseball to improve his skills, but the organization that drafted the player keeps a close watch on the player's progression. A player who is drafted as a draft-and-follow pick also has the option to accept the draft selection and sign a professional contract with the organization.

Not fully realizing what being drafted meant, I was eager to find out what professional baseball had to offer. With no recruitment letters from colleges or universities for baseball, I had no idea where my baseball career was headed. The baseball draft presented an option, so my focus was primarily on becoming a member of the Houston Astros organization. Adversely, going to college and receiving higher education was most important to Lanette. If I went to college, I would be the first male in our family to go to college. I needed to decide whether to follow her advice, or chase the Major League dream. With all the important decisions I already had to make as a high school senior, I was now blessed and cursed with an added decision.

Days after the draft ended, Mr. Wellman came to my house to talk about a possible future in professional baseball. He came inside our Hayward home and sat down on the living room couch with Lanette, Terrance and I. He came bearing gifts too. He handed all three of us brand new blue and gold Houston Astros caps. As he began to talk, he opened a pamphlet with information on the Houston Astros Minor League system. While I was excited to hear about the opportunities, my sister was skeptical of the superstar dream being sold by professional baseball. Also, she didn't want me to jump at this offer and risk missing out on the overall college experience. On the other hand, I thought my chances of playing college sports seemed slim since I hadn't been recruited by any schools. Again, my focus was on baseball, while my sister was focused on my education.

With a 3.3 high school grade point average and fair SAT scores, I had collegiate options. My scholastic achievements put me in position to attend several colleges or universities. The University of Southern California (USC) Trojans had a storied history in college sports. Attending this Los Angeles based university was the top choice of many high school students on the West Coast. With aspirations of becoming a "Man of Troy" at the USC, I went to my counselor's office to seek an application to the university. I retrieved the application, filled it out and mailed it to the Office of Admissions department at USC. While waiting on my application to process at USC, I saw a television commercial for the University of Miami, Florida. The commercial immediately grabbed my attention since I had not heard about Miami while growing up in Northern California. My lack of exposure to life outside of the Bay Area limited my knowledge of the many colleges and universities nationwide. The commercial showed pictures of students near beautiful palm trees, sandy beaches, and crystal blue ocean waters. I was instantaneously sold on Miami. The following day, I rushed to the counselor's office to request an application for admission at Miami. Once I received the application, I completed it and mailed the application to Miami marked for "Early Admission." At Miami, Early Admission was an application option that expressed a student's primary intent to attend to school. Whether accepted or denied, the student would be notified much earlier than the usual time frame for collegiate acceptance letters to be mailed out. At this time, I was set on attending Miami over USC. I just needed my acceptance letter to solidify my plans.

In June of 1997, I received mail from the University of Miami. In anticipation of their response, I opened the oversized envelope with urgency and read the letter. After reading the first sentence, I became filled with happiness and promise. I was accepted into the University of Miami, and could now attend this prestigious, private university in the fall. The University of Miami is located in Coral Gables—a small retirement town nestled about 30 minutes from infamous South Beach. I was excited about becoming a University of Miami Hurricane, and immediately started preparing to move to South Florida in the fall.

January 31, 1997

Charlton Jimerson
1563 D St Apt 1
Hayward, CA 94541-4346

Dear Charlton,

I am pleased to inform you the Admission Committee has approved your Early Action Application for Admission to study at the University of Miami. Congratulations and welcome to our family! You may begin your studies in the fall semester, August 1997, in the Computer Engineering program in the College of Engineering. The University of Miami enjoys a significant academic reputation as one of the top research and teaching institutions in the country. You will be joining an exciting academic community located in a beautiful and dynamic suburban setting.

As an Early Action candidate who has been offered admission, you should feel especially proud. Competition for admission is particularly keen in our early admission rounds. Charlton, I speak for the entire University of Miami community in saying we recognize your fine academic record and the commitment to our university you have made.

Please read carefully the enclosed information. The *Enrollment Reservation Checklist* on the following page contains important details regarding course registration, orientation, financial assistance, campus housing, and the payment of your enrollment deposit.

Lastly, please remember our offer of admission is subject to review pending the receipt of an official copy of your final high school transcript, complete with date of graduation. In the meantime, please feel free to direct any questions to the Office of Admission. Again, I offer my personal congratulations and look forward to having you as a member of our University community!

Sincerely,

Edward M. Gillis
Director of Admission

EMG/amj
Enclosures

My acceptance letter from The "U"

4TH INNING:

While living with Lanette, it felt good to remain in the same household for an extended period of time. I routinely came home, ate dinner, and slept at the same residence daily. I obeyed my curfew, kept my grades up, and stayed out of trouble during my three years at Mt. Eden. I knowingly chose to do right instead of doing wrong, even when the people around me made a different decision. If selling drugs or stealing cars was what they wanted to do, that was their decision. I was never influenced nor pressured by my peers to participate in anything criminal. After all that I had experienced, I laughed at the statistics suggesting that I would be dead or in jail based on my race, age, and household income. I had survived it all—the pain, hardship, and struggle. Sure, when times got hard I was tempted to chase the fast life. Instead, I leaned on Lanette's parental guidance and staying busy with sports to resist the temptations. At that time, I didn't realize the impact both my sister and baseball had on my future. All I knew was that I wasn't going to let myself fail.

By the summer of 1997, I hadn't been recruited by any college or university to play sports. Therefore, my plan was to go to school at the University of Miami and "walk on" to the Hurricanes baseball team. A walk-on is a player who is not recruited by the college or university to play sports. The player has taken the initiative to seek the college or university and tryout for the team. I didn't realize until much later in life the significance of walking on the baseball team at Miami. Think about some of the top-rated programs in college basketball like Duke and North Carolina. Now, imagine someone showing up there—non-recruited, walking on, and trying to make the team. This was exactly what I was up against on the baseball diamond at Miami. The best thing I had going for me was that I was unaware of the University of Miami's winning history in baseball. The only college baseball games I'd seen on local television were games played by Cal Berkeley or Stanford. Therefore, my lack of knowledge allowed me the liberty to play baseball without worrying about the high level of competition at Miami. I didn't know if I would make the team, but I believed I could compete.

When I arrived at the University of Miami, I was shocked to say the least. I was amazed by the exotic wildlife on campus. Miami is indigenous to various species of birds, including the ibis, which is the school mascot of Hurricanes. The possible threat of alligators in every lake, canal, and river was dangerously exciting to me. I often caught a glimpse of a gator in the murky waters of Lake Osceola, which centered our beautiful Miami campus. The weather remained hot like a sauna all year long. Two minutes after a shower, you could feel the sweat trickling down your back. This was tropical South Florida, and I wasted no time getting familiar with my new environment.

University of Miami Residence Housing had me set up to room with another student in the Hecht dormitory. Because I was accepted to the university based on academics, I was placed in general student housing just as any other incoming student would have been. So my sister helped me move my belongings into my new room, and afterwards I headed to the Mark Light stadium for the initial baseball team meeting. At the meeting, head coach Jim Morris spoke to the team and introduced his coaching staff to the players. The pitching coach was Lazer Collazo, a charismatic Cuban from Miami. Henry "Turtle" Thomas, a tall burly man with a country twang, was the hitting coach. The outfield and base running coach was Gino DiMare, an ex-Hurricane outfielder who was still young and energetic.

The locker room was filled with players from all across the country. As I scanned the area, I was overwhelmed by how many players were present. The locker room looked more like a football team's locker room than baseball. None of the players were introduced, yet I got a feeling for whom the returning players were. Coach Morris talked about the upcoming season and provided details on when our first official practice would be. The initial baseball team meeting was very casual.

Following the meeting, I was instructed by Coach Morris to relocate to a dorm where the other scholarship baseball players stayed. Therefore, I packed up my things and moved to the other side of campus into Mahoney Residence Hall. Derek Wigginton, an outfielder from Antioch, Tennessee, was my new roommate. Derek was a deliberately boastful young man, who wasn't afraid to mention how talented of a high school football player he used to be. He was at Miami on an athletic scholarship for baseball, but I got the feeling he missing playing on the gridiron. Looking back on it now, it's obvious that we were paired together because we were the only two Black outfielders on the team. That way, at least we could familiarize with each other based on ethnic background. Mahoney Residence Hall room 440 featured white cement walls and cold tile floors. The cot-like beds had steel frames and thin twin mattresses. There were two wooden dressers (one for each of us) and a small closet for both of us to share. The bathroom was connected to the dorm room next door, which was also occupied by baseball players. The four of us shared the bathroom with one toilet, a shower, and two sinks on each side. It wasn't a five-star hotel, but it was where we would call home as University of Miami students. With the help of Derek's parents and Lanette, we all tried to make our new living space look more like home. While putting our clothes away in drawers, and hanging posters on the wall, we talked about where we were from. With his Tennessee country twang, and my laid-back California style, we searched through conversation for common ground. At first, it was difficult trusting someone I'd just met inside my personal space and around my personal items. Especially when so many others in the past had stolen several irreplaceable items from my childhood. It's also difficult to detect if a roommate will respect your privacy—your need to study late or sleep in. Over time, Derek and I became close friends, and shared plenty of memories while at Miami. We both loved the social scene in South Florida, and neither one of us had trouble with the women.

My jersey number was #52, essentially because I was the 52nd player on the roster. There were more players on the field than there were roster spots, so it was evident to me that cuts had to be made before the team was finalized. We worked out every day of the week—running, lifting weights, hitting, or doing defensive drills. Workout times varied depending on our individual class schedules. Most players worked out in the early mornings, while others like myself sandwiched workouts between classes. I was studying Computer Engineering, which was extremely demanding for time. I carried a semester load of four courses, totaling twelve credits. My core classes were difficult and time consuming. I quickly recognized that my future depended on how well I could balance my time between baseball and academics. Dedicating sufficient time to study for school and practice baseball was tough. Many times, I arrived late to practices because my class schedule conflicted with the start times of practice. Other times, I chose to hit baseballs instead of hitting the books. I was losing sleep and skipping meals almost daily.

Fall practice was extremely competitive. Being a walk-on, it was imperative that I attract the coaching staff's attention and force them to notice my talent. I needed to play above and beyond the rest because most of my competition were scholarship players. While I had to prove myself deserving of a spot on team, others felt secure about their position. Throughout fall practice, I never knew if my performance was good enough to make the team. We played intra-squad games almost daily. On days that I played good, I felt like I would make the team. However, when I performed poorly, I assumed they would cut me after practice. As the end of fall tryouts neared, I still had a Miami jersey on my back. Each day, the names of several players were written on a board in the locker room. These players needed to go see Coach Morris in his office upstairs. Some players Coach Morris just needed to talk to, while others would be told that they had not made the team. You could tell which talk the player had just received based on his slumping shoulders or lack of eye contact upon his return downstairs. Players who were cut immediately unloaded their belongings from their locker, and departed the locker room forever. Their dream of being a University of Miami Hurricane baseball player had come to devastating end.

All my hard work in the fall was well worth it, because I made the team. Unfortunately, Derek and the two other guys from next door were not as lucky. They were all cut from the team, leaving me as the only student remaining in the two adjoining dorm rooms. Think about that for a minute, so you can get a clear picture of the situation. All three of those guys had scholarships to play at Miami and were very proud of receiving those scholarships. Yet, within months they were forced to re-evaluate their futures. Not only their futures as baseball players, but also as students. Although a school cannot rightfully take a scholarship away because a player did not make the team, it's hard to remain a student at the school after being cut. Almost every athlete who desires to play collegiate sports transfers schools after being cut from the team. Unfortunately, that decision comes with the harsh price of forfeiting a scholarship.

Although I was happy that I made the team, I was sorrowful about the players who were cut. I didn't understand why a school would do that to a kid—give them a scholarship to go to school and play ball, only to snatch it away. Maybe I was lucky to be a walk-on, and not have to be financially accounted for by the baseball program. My tuition was paid with student loans, grants, and my sister's income. When I returned home to California for Christmas holiday break, I told all my friends and family the good news. The funny thing is that most of them wanted to know which sport I was playing at Miami. People had not forgotten my basketball days at Mt. Eden. Though tempted to entertain the idea of playing basketball, I was focused on starting a very exciting baseball career at the University of Miami.

5TH INNING:

One thing I found out quickly was that I was behind in baseball development at Miami. I knew how to physically play the game, but I didn't know how to execute the fundamentals of the game. Execution is crucial in deciding wins and losses over the course of a season. For example, knowing how to hit a sacrifice fly can be the difference between winning and losing a baseball game. Coach Morris and Turtle Thomas would get on my ass about not focusing on the fundamentals of the game. I had what many call *raw* ability, meaning my skills were unfinished—like a raw steak—unprepared, and simply not ready. Thankfully, the coaching staff saw potential in me and found joy in trying to refine my baseball skills.

Throughout the season, we worked non-stop on the fundamentals of baseball during practice. First, we did drills as a team collectively, such as practicing hitting cut-offs or fielding pop-flies. We then divided the team into four groups—outfielders, infielders, pitchers, and catchers. The outfielders were with Gino, running down baseballs in the scorching South Florida heat. This was my group, and our practices consisted of fielding fly balls and ground balls for hours during the week. Gino introduced me to several outfield footwork drills that I had never seen before. In high school, I relied on my athletic ability and speed to make plays in the outfield. However, Gino taught me how to create the proper angles to the ball first, and then use my speed to catch it. He stressed the importance of being in a good starting position before the ball is put in play. He broke everything down into the very smallest detail so the movements would be fundamentally sound and flow smoothly when it was game time.

During batting practice, we worked endlessly on bunting the baseball. Both sacrifice bunting, and bunting for a base hit were important to our program. Coach Morris always believed that games could be won or lost from bunts. Games are decided by teams either not knowing how to bunt or how to defend a bunt. Being able to move a runner over to the next base from a successful bunt is vital to winning. We also worked on hitting the ball on the ground during hit-and-runs, and hitting the ball to the right side of the field to move a runner over from second base. I spent a lot of hours taking batting practice to create a natural, fluid swing. I made several adjustments to my swing throughout my first year at Miami. I altered my head position, widened my stance, and changed the way I gripped the bat. Receiving hitting instruction from Turtle Thomas allowed me to understand the concept of hitting a baseball. I took advantage of the knowledge he shared, and made changes according to his suggestions.

I was excited to start my first baseball season at Miami in February of 1998. We had some really talented players on the team like Pat Burrell, Bobby Hill, and Aubrey Huff. All three would become Major League players after leaving Miami. To compete with that group of guys and make the team was extremely challenging. Getting playing time during the season was my next challenge. I managed to play a little bit my freshman year, but at-bats were rare. I got into some games, hit a couple of home runs, and stole a few of bases. I basically just got my feet wet at the collegiate level.

That '98 season we won over fifty games and made it to the NCAA College World Series, thanks to the play of some of the people I previously mentioned. The College World Series (CWS) is an annual NCAA Collegiate Baseball double-elimination tournament played in Omaha, Nebraska. The tournament hosts the top eight teams in college baseball for that respected year. The winning team is crowned NCAA Baseball National Champion. Ever since I had arrived at Miami, all I heard everyone talk about was Omaha. The city of Omaha is synonymous with the College World Series. That year, those words became reality and I was a member of one of top eight teams in the nation.

After winning our opening game against Long Beach State 3-1, we lost our next two in a row. The two losses eliminated us from the tournament and national title contention. I remember seeing the expressions on some of the player's faces after we made our final out of our last game. Some showed their disappointment in their body language—head down and slumped shoulders. While others cried tears like a baby with no shame. I would understand later in my career that those tears were the result of suddenly realizing that their college careers had just ended. More importantly, following a game that ended with a loss on college baseball's biggest stage. At the conclusion of our season, I reflected on what had transpired in my baseball career thus far. In my first year at Miami, I walked on the baseball team and made it to the College World Series. Even though I didn't play in a game in Omaha, I was honored by the opportunity to participate in the College World Series. It was just my freshman year, therefore I was excited about my future at "The U."

In 1999, I returned to Coral Gables for my sophomore season. Over the summer, I underwent knee surgery to clean out some ligament damage from an injury that initially occurred from playing basketball in high school. Now that my knee was fixed, I bounced back feeling much stronger. I moved out of the dorm in Mahoney Residence Hall and moved into the on-campus apartments. The two-bedroom apartment—equipped with a living room, kitchen, and full bathroom—was much better than the dorms. My roommates were teammates Bobby Hill, Mike Neu, and Ryan Channel. Since Bobby Hill was also from the Bay Area, we bonded from the beginning. A huge fan of E-40 and Bone Thugs 'N Harmony, Bobby always made me laugh when he was rapping their hit music. Bobby came from a loving Mexican family that frequently traveled to Miami to support Bobby's promising baseball career. He was a star shortstop at Miami, and would later play Major League baseball for the Chicago Cubs and Pittsburgh Pirates. I loved spending time with the Hill family whenever they visited Miami. They always cooked authentic, home-cooked Mexican food for the house whenever they were in town.

A new wave of players joined the Hurricanes baseball team in 1999. Among them included a dynamic duo of freshman outfielders. The first was Chicago native Marcus Nettles, who was rumored to be one of the fastest guys in college baseball. Marcus was 5'11, with a muscular build, and athletic as hell. He maintained an angry demeanor until he decided to reveal his contagious smile and laughter. He was a talker, who had the gift of gab to steal a lady's heart, or capture a room full of corporate executives. The other addition to the outfield was Mike Rodriguez, an extremely talented left-handed hitter from Ft. Lauderdale. Mike was Cuban-American, which made him much more dynamic than most. His charismatic Cuban father was often seen chatting with the coaching staff. He regularly brought players and coaches Cuban cigars as gifts. His mother was a soft-spoken, fair-skinned woman with beautiful curly red hair. Mike drew from both of his parent's personality traits. He was interactive and social one minute, but reclusive and secluded the next. As outfielders, Marcus, Mike, and I naturally grew close as friends. We spent a lot of time together in the locker room, on the field, and hanging out on campus. Even though my playing time was reduced significantly after their arrival, I maintained a genuine friendship with the both of them.

My sophomore season was pretty much spent backing up these two freshmen, who wasted no time showing they were prepared to play. They both had played more organized baseball in the past, and benefitted from better coaching during that time. To be honest, they were simply more prepared to play Division I college baseball than I was. It was something I had to accept, but not settle for. At some point, every player must concede that another player is better. There is nothing more pitiful than a player who cannot own the reality that someone else's skills are superior. Instead of working harder to get better in the future, they hate on the competition, thinking that will hide their own deficiencies. Maybe someone else has better skills now, but if you work hard at your craft and improve, then you can propel yourself ahead of the competition. Basically, use the unsatisfied feeling of being a bench player as fuel for progression. I took my own advice. Instead of hating on them, I left it all up to good 'ole competition. We battled it out every day in practice and games. Each of us trying to win the favor of Coach Morris over the next man. The friendly competition we had at Miami as outfielders strengthened our friendship off the field. The competition also propelled our team to an historic season. We returned to the College World Series and stormed into the tournament boasting a 46-13 record.

Since I had experienced the College World Series a year ago, I was already accustomed to the emotions of Omaha. The feeling of anxiety, the media attention, and signing autographs for fans were all familiar to me. Only this time, I couldn't wait to get on the field and contribute. Throughout the regular season, I backed up Mike and Marcus in the outfield. I entered almost every game in the late innings to play left, right, or center field. My specialty was my defense at any outfield position. The ability to play all outfield positions increased my chances of playing in games. During the regular season, I frequently entered the game as a pinch runner. I was a highly skilled base stealer, so I would steal a base for the team in late innings when needed. Behind Marcus and Mike, I was the next faster player on the team. If I was lucky, I got a chance to bat in the games that I played in. But many times, the game would end prior to my turn in the lineup. Even though I occasionally started games in the outfield during the season, I wasn't expecting to start in Omaha. I figured I would maintain the same role in the College World Series that I had played all season long. However, we won game one...and I didn't play. We won game two...and I didn't play. We won game three and game four... and I didn't fucking play! We were crowned 1999 NCAA Collegiate Baseball National Champions, but for the second consecutive year, I never got to play in a game at the College World Series.

Following the championship game, it took every bit of me to not react selfishly. I attempted to be excited for the team, but deep inside I was dejected by the fact that I never got a chance to play. We won, but I didn't feel like I was a part of us winning. While everyone else was celebrating our victory, I forcefully squeezed out smiles. I understood how my contributions were important to our overall team success. However, I didn't feel as valuable because I didn't hit, throw, or catch a single baseball in a game at the College World Series. To make matters worse, I didn't even get a chance to run the bases. I was so frustrated that I called home that same day and told my sister that I wanted to transfer schools. Lanette didn't want to hear my complaining. She told me to stick with it, not to give up, and stay positive for the future. She reminded me that success doesn't come easy for something you really want. She was worried about my current state of baseball depression, but most importantly, I recall her concern for my safety. Her motherly instinct was driving her to advise me to stay at Miami. She didn't feel comfortable with me moving to another college city, when she already knew I was safe in Coral Gables. I remember her saying that my time to shine was coming. I wonder if she had a premonition of what would happen in the future. I trusted my sister's advice and remained enrolled at Miami for my junior year.

Still upset about not playing in the College World Series in 1999, my baseball frustration at Miami only grew in 2000. Entering my junior year, my reputation as a baseball player at Miami was personally displeasing. I was commonly labeled as a bench player that was known for striking out, and only worthy of late-inning game appearances. I didn't want that to be my permanent label as a player. At the very least, I wanted to be remembered as a quality outfielder, since I'd always played good defense throughout my college career. Marcus and Mike also returned as sophomore outfielders with the same edge they had on me a year ago. Therefore, I was subjected to yet another year of being on the bench. Because I wasn't a starter, I took every day of batting practice seriously. In the outfield, I perfected my skills by chasing balls down—climbing on the fence, diving on the grass, doing whatever it took to catch the ball. I didn't care that it was *just* batting practice. These practices were my game time, since I knew I wasn't in the starting lineup. Even though I was solid on defense, my hitting was blinding people from seeing anything other than the strikeouts. To make matters worse, about a month before the season started, I suffered two stress fractures in my lower back. I wore a back brace for a month, which slowed my baseball development. It was probably the worst season I've had my entire baseball career and certainly the worst as a college player. I basically wasted a year of my eligibility, due to injuries and insufficient play on the field. The 2000 season at Miami was a strenuous period in my baseball career. Although my immediate future in baseball seemed bleak, I knew I still had one year of eligibility remaining. There was still time to right the ship and leave my mark at the University of Miami.

Despite baseball hitting rock bottom, my social life at Miami was at its peak. I met a bunch of people from all over the country, including Southern California, New York, and Atlanta. Guys like Francisco "Cisco" Navarro, Robert "Shamu" Fernandez, Elan "Big E" Jennings, and Gary "G" Pinnock were guys whom I befriended while at Miami. Not to mention all the Caribbean people I met from Jamaica, the Bahamas, and the Virgin Islands. Never before had I seen such beautiful Black people not born in the United States. That is one of the reasons why I loved living in South Florida. It was a melting pot of all types of cultures just like the Bay Area. On campus, I gained notoriety for throwing the most mind-blowing house parties at Miami. At least twice a semester, I hosted a "West Coast Party" at my apartment. My new room-mates Marcus Nettles and Jamin Thompson helped me orchestrate the par-ties. For each party, students packed into my apartment to partake in dancing and drinking. We partied until the walls were literally sweating. The location of my apartment was perfectly tucked away from campus traffic. The mini-mal traffic in our area reduced the possibility for the party to be shut down by campus police for being too loud. Therefore, my house parties didn't stop 'til the wee hours of the night. University of Miami students love to party, so partying until the sun rises is common. The Miami Hurricane football play-ers were also guests at my parties. Future NFL stars Andre Johnson of the Houston Texans, Reggie Wayne of the Indianapolis Colts, and Clinton Portis of the Washington Redskins were familiar faces at my parties. They were all there to ogle at the masses of beautiful women whom attended my parties. It was vital to my mental state for me to enjoy life outside of baseball. Especially during that time when playing baseball wasn't very gratifying.

Even though I was playing baseball at an elite private university, I was strug-gling to keep my head above water. My student loans were increasing in amount, school books weren't getting any cheaper, and the general cost of living in Miami was expensive. I remember days when I was starving, but my meals account or "Cane Card" was in the negative. I used to call home to Lanette and ask her if she could put $20 in my bank account so I could buy something to eat. Back then, the McDonald's across the street from my apartment had a special—cheeseburgers were only 39 cents on Wednesdays. I stacked up on cheeseburgers so that I would have food for the next day or so. I wasn't the only athlete struggling to make ends meet while attending a prestigious college or university. Many athletes nationwide experienced the same struggles that I did, or worst. It's sad that college athletes can essentially make a school millions of dollars by their performance on the field, yet struggle to feed themselves on a daily basis. Sure, college athletes are provided meals as a part of their scholarship or tuition. But those meals don't cover all dining situations, such as the cafeteria being closed. From personal experience, I can understand the recent pleas for college athletes to be compensated for playing their sport. Placing responsibility on a starving seventeen year old kid to decide how to financially support himself or his family, opens the door for possible violations. A player will almost certainly do whatever it takes to fight going hungry, even if it means risking their eligibility. Surprisingly, to my knowledge, there are no resources available for a financially challenged athlete to utilize. The NCAA should do more to provide assistance to college athletes who have a financial need that exceeds their budget. I suggest that the NCAA introduce the "I'M A BROKE ATHLETE" grant to be available for all financially challenged college athletes...just saying.

When my senior year approached, I knew it was time to get serious. It was time for me to show others that I had what it takes to play baseball at the collegiate level. There was no coming back to college for another year to play baseball after this season was over. Good thing was I was healthy again, which was gratifying since injuries had troubled me the previous season. All I needed to do was mentally prepare to handle whatever I would encounter my senior year. I had experienced so many different emotions and feelings in my first three years at Miami. It was absolutely necessary for me to balance those emotions throughout my senior season.

Before each season began, each player filled out a goal sheet and listed both individual and team goals for the season. The goal sheets included what we needed to work on individually, and what our team goals were for the season. After the goal sheets were all completed, each player had a personal one-on-one meeting with Coach Morris to review their goal sheet. Each year I set my goals overly high. At the end of the season, I would be significantly short of achieving my goals. I believed that if I set my goals extremely high and strived for them every day, ultimately I was successful even if I didn't reach my target. Despite falling short, I achieved more by chasing my high goals than I would have by settling for mediocre goals. For example, if I set out to have a .300 batting average for the season, and only hit .280, I would be satisfied with my performance because I was pushing for .300 the whole time. But, had I only tried to hit .260 (which was a very attainable goal), I'd be selling myself short. I might reach my goal and hit .260, but I possibly could have hit .280 if I had set my goals higher. I always achieved more by having something arduous to attain, rather than set goals that I already knew I could reach. I continued to set goals with the same mindset throughout my baseball career.

It was arguably insane how high I'd set my personal goals for my senior year at Miami. I aimed to become a starter, hit .300 for the season, and be drafted in the first round of the 2001 MLB Draft. The previous year I was on the bench almost every game, hit a measly .206 in 68 at-bats, and went undrafted. No doubt, I knew my goals were practically impossible. It was all on me to make something happen. I started out the season as a backup bench player, just like every other year at Miami. Most of time, I only got one at-bat in games which I played, so I knew I had to take advantage of minimal opportunities. It was important that I have good, quality at-bats at the plate to increase my playing time as the season progressed. I was a better player, and it was all on me to show it whenever I got a chance to play.

Playing off the bench continued until our big series against Florida State. That's when Marcus, our starting left fielder, pulled his hamstring muscle. With the injury, he would be out for at least two weeks, so my opportunity to get sufficient playing time had arrived. Though I was more anxious than nervous, I was absolutely elated about my new role as a starter. Although I knew I was in the starting lineup, I wondered where I would hit in the batting order. Since I was exceptionally gifted defensively, I didn't care what position I played on defense. All I could focus on was finally getting my chance to get three or four at-bats in a game. This was no ordinary game neither—this was Florida State weekend, so the level of anticipation was immensely magnified. The Florida State Seminoles (FSU) were our most despised rivals, and bitter enemies. They hated us, and we hated them. Back then, both schools were college powerhouses in both baseball and football. Therefore, the malicious relationship between Miami and Florida State was heightened every time we played each other. There wasn't a team on our entire schedule that I would rather play against than Florida State. I could not have planned it any better.

For the first game against Florida State, Coach Morris had me playing center field and hitting leadoff. My opportunity to retain a starting spot in the Hurricanes lineup had arrived. It was up to me to seize the moment, and that's exactly what I did. Since we were the visiting team, I was the first batter of the game. In my first at-bat, I hit a scorching home run to left field. My first at-bat set the tone for an overall outstanding series. In three games against the Seminoles, I had several multi-hit games and caught almost everything hit to the outfield. Not to mention being a terror on the base paths, and stealing bases at will. As a hitter, it's important to get off to a good start in the game. Even if you don't get a hit, it's crucial to see a lot of pitches or hit the ball hard somewhere. That first at-bat gave me the confidence I needed to believe in myself. We swept FSU in the three-game series—which was something that rarely happened in Tallahassee, Florida—home of Seminoles.

CATCH ME IF YOU CAN! DOING WORK ON THE DIAMOND

Now that I had a starting spot, there was no room to slack off in my performance. I knew that if I didn't want to return to the bench, I had to maintain my level of play established in Tallahassee. Therefore, I approached every game and practice with the utmost intensity that I could maintain each day. I had to keep working on my game until everyone believed that I was the real deal. Over the next few weeks, I continued to collect hits and steal bases as a starter. Therefore, by the time Marcus was back healthy and ready to play, Coach Morris didn't change the lineup. I was playing too good to put me back on the bench. I had made believers out of the same people who doubted me. I never relinquished my starting spot in the outfield. I played rest of the season as the University of Miami Hurricanes center fielder.

Although excited about being a starter, I hated being in competition with Marcus. My roommate and close friend was now sitting the bench. In my eyes, the both of us could have roamed the outfield together. Instead, it was set up to be an unnecessary competition between friends. Fortunately, Marcus and I had a strong bond off the field. Our friendship allowed the both of us to support each other on the field, regardless of who was starting. We had our eyes set on a winning another national championship.

We returned to the NCAA tournament in 2001. We were the host team for the South Region. In Regionals, we beat Bucknell (14-6), Florida (6-2) and Stetson (16-8) in front of our home crowd in Coral Gables. Next, we hosted the Super Regionals for the South Region. The new Super Regional format was a best two-out-of-three weekend series. In the Super Regional, we hosted the Clemson Tigers. We wasted no time finishing off Clemson, needing only two games to win the series. The wins clinched us yet another College World Series berth.

The 2001 Major League Baseball Amateur Draft was held days after our Super Regional win. Every player on the team was fully aware of the importance of the draft, since almost all of us had been previously drafted. In fact, many players only attended Miami because of the increased probability of being drafted higher three or four years later. Everyone knew that the higher you were picked in the draft, the higher the signing bonus amount you could receive. Because of our winning history, many players shared the Major League draft spotlight. Major League scouts are attracted to winning teams, because if a team is winning, the players on the team must be playing the game the right way. As a team, we understood that when a team is successful, the individuals on that team get increased recognition. On draft day, most of my draft eligible teammates sat in front of their computers surfing the internet. Players were eagerly awaiting web postings and updates about the draft on the internet. At that time, the internet was the fastest way to know who had been drafted and in what round.

Instead of being confined to a computer screen awaiting draft results, I went to eat lunch at Johnny Rockets. I'm not saying I wasn't interested to know if I had been drafted, I just didn't want to look like I was! While enjoying a bacon double cheeseburger, my cell phone rang. I casually reached for my phone to answer it. Moments later, I received notification that I had been drafted by the Houston Astros...again. The Astros selected me in the fifth round of the 2001 MLB Draft (146th overall) just four years after drafting me in the twenty-fourth round (760th overall) out of high school. I increased my draft position by over 600 selections since the Astros drafted me in 1997. I was beyond happy knowing that if I wanted, there was more baseball to be played after the College World Series.

Back in the locker room, I could tell from the look on the faces of several teammates, which players went undrafted. The disappointment was written all over their face. Hopefully, their disappointment over the draft would not be a distraction on the field. As a college player, it can be hard to focus on baseball when you feel like you have been overlooked by professional baseball scouts. Even those who feel they should have been drafted higher can be distracted by the draft. It can become a problem for teams whose star players aren't giving their full effort because of their bitterness in how the draft panned out.

As a senior, I realized that I was either going to get drafted, or I wasn't. Unlike underclassmen, I didn't have bargaining power. College juniors have the option to accept or decline a Major League contract from the team which drafted them. They can also lobby for more money towards their signing bonus. If they don't like where they were selected in the draft, or the amount offered, they can opt to return to school for their senior year. My draft status was not negotiable, so I didn't care where I was selected in the draft. Therefore, the results of the 2001 MLB Draft didn't disrupt my baseball mentality. I was just grateful that I was blessed with the opportunity to play professional baseball.

I always wondered why the draft wasn't held after the College World Series. Holding the draft after the College World Series would allow players to complete their college career free from any distraction related to professional baseball. Then, if drafted, players can switch their focus to professional baseball. If there was a genuine relationship between the NCAA and Major League Baseball (MLB), the draft would never overlap college baseball. Coach Morris protected his players by demanding MLB scouts to respect the players' task at hand. Winning a NCAA national championship was top priority at the moment. Professional baseball could wait until after the College World Series was over.

Chuck Carlson, the Houston Astros scout responsible for drafting me, respectfully allowed me to focus on college baseball. Mr. Carlson, like many other MLB scouts, was in Omaha to watch the multitude of drafted players. He wanted to personally welcome me to the Houston Astros organization. Mr. Carlson and I met in the lobby of the team hotel and conversed briefly. He told me to concentrate on winning a ring, and we would discuss my future with the Astros when the time was right. He made an impactful first impression, courtesy of the Houston Astros Baseball Club. From that day forward, Chuck and I were bonded by the 2001 MLB draft. I was like one of his sheep, and he was my shepherd. He would continue to guide me throughout my baseball career.

Our first game of the College World Series was against the University of Tennessee Volunteers. Although this was my third trip to the College World Series, I had yet to play in a game in Omaha. I was excited about the opportunity to play this year, and possibly contribute to a national title. I had a great group of teammates that could play the game exceptionally well. Kevin Howard, Kevin Brown, Tom Farmer, and Brian Walker were some of the guys who carried our team. Knowing that I had talented teammates helped take some of the pressure off myself to perform. I had teammates that were more than willing to share the responsibility. We were a family, committed to do whatever it takes to win. Before the game started, I had to check the starting lineup card just to make sure I was playing. I had not forgotten that twice before I came and left Omaha without playing. Those horrible feelings of years past in Omaha were still affecting me.

As game time approached, I began to soak it all in. The smell of hot dogs wafted through Rosenblatt Stadium as fans packed the stadium. The sun was shining brightly off the Omaha Zoo's dome-shaped, metallic building located behind right field. The playing surface had an aura of excitement. Something special was about to happen, maybe even something historic. The electric atmosphere ignited a fiery emotion to build inside of me. I felt the same kind of feeling that a Roman gladiator must have felt before a match at the Colosseum. I was ready to battle on the biggest stage of college baseball and show everybody that I could play. We were the visiting team against the Volunteers, so just like in Tallahassee, I would be the first batter of the game. When Tennessee took the field, there was a loud applause from the crowd. Wyatt Allen, the ace of the Volunteers pitching staff and first round draft selection of the Chicago White Sox, took the mound. It was game time.

As they announced my name over the public announcement system, I strolled up to home plate to hit. I stepped in the batter's box, and before I realized it, the pitcher had already thrown three pitches. In what seemed like seconds, I was behind in the count one ball and two strikes. The game was moving so fast that I had to calm myself down and relax. I stepped out of the batter's box and took a deep breath. I returned to the batter's box and regained my focus. I was ready now for his next delivery. Allen hurled his next pitch, and I smacked it over the left-center field wall for a home run. I glared into the outfield in amazement as I ran the bases, shocked that I just led off the game with a home run. It was unreal. I felt like my body was running fast, but my mind was moving in slow motion at the same time. My adrenaline was rushing, I was pouring with sweat, and I felt like screaming. Standing near second base was shortstop Chris Burke, 2001 first round draft pick for the Houston Astros. As I ran towards second base I yelled out "Woooooooooo! Wooooooooo! Let's

Go Baby!!" With my braids flowing out of the back of my helmet, I was float-
ing on air. Coming around third base, coach Gino DiMare was standing in
the third base foul line, waiting to give me a high five. Meanwhile, all my
teammates were gathered near home plate, jumping around and cheering in
excitement. That's how we did it at Miami. Whenever we went deep, we celebrated as a team at home plate to make sure the pitcher knew we appreciated
the offering. If you don't like us celebrating at home plate, then don't let us hit
home runs.

THE CELEBRATION AFTER LEADING OFF THE GAME WITH A HOME RUN

That was the first of many runs scored in that game, as both teams went on
to score a combined 34 runs. We won by a final score of 21-13. At that time, it
was the longest game played in College World Series history. The game was 4:
21 minutes of baseball being battled to the last out. I think both teams understood the importance of winning the first game of the series. In a double-elimination format, it's difficult to win the tournament after losing the first game.

After our victory against Tennessee, I received interview requests from a slew of reporters. There were camera crews and newspaper reporters everywhere trying to get a story on me. They all wanted to know: *who was this exciting player that utterly came out of nowhere?* In the midst of all the attention and interviews, I remained focused on playing the game. Although I enjoyed the spotlight, I wanted the focus to be on our team. I was looking forward to our next game against the University of Southern California Trojans. Southern California was the school I wanted to attend and play for coming out of high school. I desperately wanted to beat them to show them that they made a mistake by not accepting my application.

In a business where you're only as good as your last game, it was time to show and prove myself again. The University of Southern California baseball team was stacked with talent, including an exceptional pitching staff. Starting pitcher Mark Prior, the number two overall pick in the 2001 MLB draft, was Southern California's ace. Taking the mound for the game against us was Rick Currier, a crafty right-hander who had already won twelve games that season. Although still a bit nervous, I entered this game a little bit more relaxed than the previous one. My undeniable desire to compete trumped my nervous anxiety. In my first at-bat, with two balls and two strikes, Currier tossed me a slider and I crushed it. The ball flew deep over the right-center field wall and crashed into the scoreboard. The ball hit the display screen, which had my headshot profile showing during my at-bat. I indirectly hit myself with the ball! It was the second game in a row that I had led off with a home run, setting a College World Series record. I still hold the record today for most leadoff home runs in a College World Series.

Most importantly, my home run gave our team the early lead for the second consecutive game. The score of the game remained 1-0 until the fifth inning. In the top of the fifth with two outs, USC's third baseman Brian Barre hit a deep fly ball to right-center field. When the ball was hit, I was playing in center field, but positioned more towards left field. Therefore, I had to "get on my horse" if I wanted to catch the batted ball. I ran full speed while tracking the ball in the air as it soared towards the outfield wall. With the wall approaching, I had a decision to make. Either I stop running and hope the ball hit the wall and bounced off, or keep running and make a leap for the ball in the air. I measured my steps, jumped in the air, and reached for the ball as far as my glove would allow.

"THE CATCH"

While in the air, I thought I felt something inside my glove but I wasn't sure if I had caught the ball. When I came down, I looked in my glove, and there it was. As outfielders, many times we feel like we have caught the ball, only to look in our glove and find nothing there. Once I saw the ball, I put both hands in the air and sprinted towards the dugout in excitement.

THE EXCITEMENT AFTER MAKING THE CATCH

The stadium went wild. Everyone was astonished at the play I just made in such a close game. The excitement from my defensive play catapulted our offense in the bottom of the fifth, as we added three runs to our lead. Thanks to our team defense, we held on to win a phenomenal game by the final score of 4-3. After the game, the locker room was packed with reporters who wanted to interview me. There were reporters from all over the country, including sports columnists from Northern California and South Florida. There were also reporters from national publications such as USA Today. In addition to interviews with newspaper reporters, I was also wanted for a post-game interview with official NCAA College World Series media. I finished answering all questions from reporters in the locker room, then proceeded to walk to the post-game media room. I was joined by several other teammates and Coach Morris.

The post-game media room was located below the concourse level at Rosenblatt Stadium. When we arrived at the media room, I was shocked by how similar it was to a Major League Baseball press conference room. Huddled in the back of the room was a group of reporters, patiently awaiting our arrival. Towards the front of the room stood a long row of tables, covered in blue tablecloth, and full of microphones. There was a microphone and a nameplate placed in front of each seat to designate seating arrangements. Both players and coaches were available for questioning, but it seemed like everyone wanted to talk to me. Never in my life had I been in a place where so many people wanted to talk to me. Everyone wanted to know about my baseball background and even more about my personal life. At that time, not many people knew the things that I had experienced in my lifetime. Information—some of it wrong—about the childhood troubles that I endured started to surface, and the topic quickly became the lead story. The questions didn't bother me much. I just hoped that the focus would stay more on how well I was playing baseball, and less about how *traumatic* life was for me growing up. People were inspired by my journey, so I was happy my story would be broadcasted across the nation. But, there was an immeasurable amount of distasteful Jimerson news articles—embellished by the imagination of the media—that were disappointing for me to read. As I've mentioned before, nobody can tell my story better than me, not even the most resourceful of reporters.

The University of Tennessee was our opponent in game three, the second time we faced them in this round robin, double-elimination tournament. Since Tennessee had already lost a game, and we were undefeated, they needed to beat us twice to advance. While all we had to do was win one game against the Volunteers to advance to the College World Series championship game. We knew Tennessee was a tough squad because of the first game we had played against each other. That game was such a high scoring match, that it could have gone either way. Game three began in Tennessee's favor in the early innings. The Volunteer offense jumped on our starting pitcher, Kiki Bengochea, scoring four runs in the first three innings. The fourth inning was our breakthrough inning. Mike Rodriguez led off the top of the fourth with a single, Javy Rodriguez bunted for a hit, and then Kevin Howard smashed a three-run home run. The next batter, Kevin Mannix, was hit by a pitch, and Kevin Brown followed with a double. Two batters later, with two outs, I lined a single to left field. Now with runners on first and second base, the next batter Mike Rodriguez hit a missile over the second baseman's head. When Rodriguez hit the ball, I took off running top speed towards second base. Prior to reaching second base, I glanced over at Gino to see if I should keep running towards third base. He was waving his hands hysterically, directing me to keep going to third base. As I approached third base, I looked at Gino to see if he wanted me to stop at third base, or head for home plate. I did not see his hands up indicating me to stop, so I rounded third base and dashed for home. The only problem was, Gino wanted me to stay at third base. Either he was late putting his hands up to signal me to stop, or I had disregarded his hand signals altogether. By this time, the Tennessee outfielder had recovered the ball and threw it to the second baseman. The second baseman caught the ball, turned towards home plate, and fired the ball to the catcher hovering over home plate. As the ball approached, I positioned myself to slide head first into home plate, away from the catcher. Just as the catcher caught the ball, I swiped home plate with my hand, and avoided being tagged by the catcher. I looked up as the umpire yelled, "Safe!!" After hearing the call, I jumped up in total elation. My teammates stormed towards home plate to celebrate. Again, if you don't want to see us celebrating, then don't let us score.

JUST BARELY BEAT THE TAG AT HOME PLATE

The runs we scored in the fourth inning gave our team a demanding 7-2 lead. The excitement from my nail-biting play at the plate astonished the crowd and propelled our team. We won the game 12-6, and eliminated Tennessee from the College World Series. The win sent us to the championship game to play against the winner of Stanford and California State Fullerton. For the second time in the last three years, the Miami Hurricanes were back in the College World Series title game. I was excited for our team and proud of my performance at the College World Series. I was playing the game of baseball with no fear, like the kid who used to play strikeout on the block. My coaching staff had prepared me to play the game hard, and play the game smart.

Stanford would later advance to the championship game, by beating California State Fullerton by the score of 4-1. The championship match was now set between Miami and Stanford, two highly respected college baseball programs. Stanford had a team full of remarkable freshman and sophomore players. On the other hand, we were the more experienced team because we had players on our roster that had already won a national championship. Being from the Bay Area, I was excited to play against Stanford. Their campus is nestled in Palo Alto, California, just thirty minutes from where I grew up. The city is normally mentioned in the same sentence with computer technology. Most of the early development and success of Silicon Valley was created within the city limits of Palo Alto. A reporter once asked me at the College World Series why I wasn't recruited by Southern California or Stanford. I didn't know the answer to that question, but I wanted to make both schools pay for not pursuing me.

The championship game wasn't until Saturday June 16th, 2001, two days after our victory over Tennessee. The break in action gave our team some time to refresh and prepare for the title match. The time also allowed my sister and Coach Muniz ample time to travel to Nebraska and watch the championship game. While my sister caught a flight from Oakland to Omaha, Ted opted to team up with his friend for a road trip. They drove 1,600 miles at whatever speed necessary to arrive in Omaha by game time on Saturday. No one on the planet was more proud of my success than Lanette and Ted. Not simply because of what I did on the field, but also because of what I had accomplished in life. There were both so proud that I was only twelve credits away from my Bachelor of Science degree in Computer Science & Mathematics. They both valued education and understood how challenging it was for me to balance both academics and athletics. They were just as proud of my success in school as they were of my success in baseball. When they arrived in Omaha, I felt a sense of completeness. I was now ready to play in the championship game.

When I laid down to sleep the night before the game, I imagined what winning the game would feel like. I wondered how I would play, who would be the hero, and how we would celebrate after the last out was made. Although I knew that losing was a possibility, I was confident in our team that we would be victorious. I said my prayers, closed my eyes, and went to sleep. I'm the kind of person who can lay their thoughts to rest. At some point, I go to sleep knowing that tomorrow will produce the opportunity for me to simply do my best.

When I woke up in the morning, I tried to convince myself that June 16th, 2001 was just another game day. Instead, I was a bit apprehensive since I had never played in a game of this magnitude. Since it was a day game, we had to be up early in the morning for our team breakfast. We ate buffet-style breakfast in one of the conference ballrooms of our team hotel. There were pancakes, eggs, bacon and sausages, fruit, juice and more. They served us food that was fit for a king, therefore I ate like one. I have never been one to pass up a good meal, especially not before a game. After we finished breakfast as a team, we all packed up the team bus and headed for Rosenblatt Stadium.

The weather was perfect on that summer day in Omaha, Nebraska. The sun was shining, the sky was clear blue, and there was an occasional cool breeze blowing through the stadium. On the mound for Stanford was left-hander Mike Gosling, a second round draft pick by the Arizona Diamondbacks. Throwing for us was our opening game winner, Tom Farmer, who had surprised many this season with his pitching success. The championship game started as a back and forth pitcher's duel, with no runs scored in the first two innings. Farmer commenced the battle by holding Stanford scoreless in the first and second innings. Gosling countered by not allowing a runner to advance past second base. The anxiety from both dugouts was overwhelming, as both teams wondered who would go ahead first and take the lead. Almost every player was standing on the top step of the dugout, with their elbows resting atop the foam-cushioned fence. Their attention riveted to every movement on the field.

The game changed in our favor in the bottom of the third inning. With runners on first and second base, and no outs, designated hitter Danny Matienzo hit a high fly ball to right field. The Stanford right fielder and future Major Leaguer Carlos Quentin battled the sun in attempt to make the catch. But he misjudged the catch and the ball dropped in right field. The runner at second base scored on the play and the runner at first base advanced all the way to third base. It was the first run scored in the game, which meant we had drawn first blood. The next batter Kevin Howard walked to load up the bases. Then Kevin Mannix doubled, allowing three more runs to score. Our dugout exploded with excitement after Mannix drove in those runs. We understood how crucial it was to get some runs early in a game where scoring could be difficult. In baseball, it's tough to come back and win a game after being down four runs in the early innings. After scoring in the third inning, Tom Farmer went to the mound and threw two more scoreless innings to keep Stanford in check. In the bottom of the fifth inning, our offense added five more runs, giving us a 9-0 lead over Stanford. Bullpen pitchers Luke Dibold, and Alex Prendes followed Farmer's performance, by only allowing one run over the next four frames. We dominated Stanford in all facets of the game. As a team, they looked beat down, broken-hearted, and dejected. On the other hand, our players were ecstatic about being in great position to win another title.

With two outs in the ninth inning, Stanford hitter Darin Naatjes popped the ball up towards second base. As soon as he hit it, I began running towards the infield with my hands in the air. I knew from the flight of the ball that the game was over. Our shortstop Javy Rodriguez reeled it in and we all charged the mound, jumping in excitement as we all dog piled on top of each other. We did it again! We were the 2001 NCAA Collegiate Baseball Champions.

MIAMI HURRICANES: 2001 NCAA COLLEGIATE
BASEBALL NATIONAL CHAMPIONS

After celebrating amongst each other on the field with hugs and hand-shakes, many of the players headed towards the stands. They wanted to acknowledge the people who had supported them along the way. I went to the stands to hug my sister, the woman who had made of all this possible. As I approached her, she was crying tears of joy. Many of the other parents were shedding tears of joy as well. Minutes later, our fans began chanting, "It's great...to be...a Miami Hurricane!!" It was an amazing experience winning my second National Championship. The feelings I had after winning in 2001 were completely different than my reaction in 1999. This time, I was filled with the great joy of knowing that I was a main contributor to us winning a championship. And this moment would only become more special.

The NCAA Collegiate Baseball National Championship trophy was presented to our team on the field. Coach Morris accepted this trophy from NCAA officials on behalf of the University of Miami. After the presentation, NCAA officials notified me that I was voted the Most Outstanding Player of the College World Series. For this honor, I was awarded a huge and extremely heavy bronze trophy. It was a miniature replica of "The Road to Omaha" statue located just outside the stadium. The 16-inch trophy features players celebrating in victory at the College World Series. It favored the Heisman Trophy—an award given to college football's most outstanding player annually. I was both honored and thankful that the committee voted for me. It was the perfect ending to all the hard work, pain, and hardships I had experienced during my career at Miami. All the years I'd been in the background, working hard, while trying to stay positive to keep the focus on the team. Now I was in the spotlight, yet I still kept the focus on the team. We fought this battle together, from the first day of practice to the last out at the College World Series. Now the curtains had closed on the biggest stage in college baseball, and this would be the final performance of my college career.

"ROAD TO OMAHA" TROPHY PRESENTED TO THE COLLEGE
WORLD SERIES MOST OUTSTANDING PLAYER

That night we celebrated like rock stars in Omaha. We partied at our team hotel all night, drinking liquor and listening to music in our rooms. While some of the players had their girlfriends in town, most did not. For those players that did not, the Miami baseball cheerleaders or "Sugar Canes" were pleasant company. The Sugar Canes were a group of female University of Miami students who volunteered to work home baseball games. They picked up our baseball bats, and brought the umpire new baseballs during the game. Not to mention, the Sugar Canes were a collection of very attractive females too. The Sugar Canes also often traveled, on their own dime, to road baseball games. Many of the Sugar Canes had made the trip to Omaha to cheer on their beloved Hurricanes. They were staying at the same hotel as the team, so we all hung out together after the game. We combined baseball players, cheerleaders, and alcohol to create the perfect recipe for celebrating our national championship.

6ᵀᴴ INNING:

A week after the College World Series ended, Chuck Carlson flew out to Hayward and met up with Gene Wellman. Since Mr. Carlson had never been to the Bay Area, he leaned on Mr. Wellman's guidance while in town. The two of them drove to my house together with the intention of discussing my contract. Although I had briefly met with Mr. Carlson in Omaha, I was nervous with anticipation about their arrival. I normally know people a lot better before inviting them in my house. I did not know Mr. Carlson or Mr. Wellman well enough to feel comfortable with them in my home. Not allowing people inside my personal space is a learned personality trait that directly relates to my troubled upbringing. Growing up, I remained cautious of the people who entered my home.

At the time, I was living with my sister and her fiancé in their beautiful home atop the Hayward Hills. I heard a knock on the door and when I opened it, Chuck Carlson and Gene Wellman stood outside motionless. Mr. Carlson looked me directly in my eyes and asked, "Is Charlton home?" I laughed and replied, "It's me, Chuck!" Since my last game in Omaha, I'd cut off my braided hair that had become my signature style at Miami. So when Mr. Carlson saw me, he had no clue that I was the person he was looking for. After enjoying another laugh, I invited them both inside and introduced them to my family.

After everyone got acquainted, Lanette and I sat down with our guests to review my baseball contract. The contract was worth more money than I had ever seen in my life. It also included money set aside for me to go back to school and finish my college degree. The Major League Baseball Scholarship Plan was an educational program specifically designed for players who wanted to go to school after baseball. For example, a high school player who signs a professional contract can get the plan added to their contact. With the plan, players can attend college after baseball, which included the off-season. The money can only be used towards their education. Expenses such as tuition, room and board, and most school associated fees are covered by the plan. Adding the plan was very important to Lanette. She continually stressed the importance of receiving higher education and completing my degree. The plan gave me the opportunity to finish my degree in Computer Science. Many times, people have the resources to assist them in receiving higher education, but fail to take advantage. I promised myself that I would finish my degree at the University of Miami.

Being a student-athlete was something that was drilled in our heads while at Miami. Coach Morris pinpointed the unique combination of the words student and athlete. The term encapsulates being both a student and athlete concurrently, without sacrificing performance on either side. And by nature of its format, emphasis is placed on being a student first. That's why it is called student-athlete, instead of athlete-student. The scholarship program reinforced what I was taught while at Miami. After we all agreed to the terms of my contract, I signed the contract and became a member of the Houston Astros organization.

In professional baseball, the road to the Major Leagues has many stops along the way. These stops are called the Minor Leagues. The Minor Leagues have different levels of competition, which are used as developmental checkpoints for the players. These levels are designated by class, going in order beginning at Rookie, Single-A Low, Single-A High, Double-A, and Triple-A. The teams playing at these levels act as stepping stones to the Major Leagues. Players will play on these teams at different levels until the organization feels that the player is ready for the Major Leagues. There is no mandatory level to be completed along the road to the Majors. Players can skip levels and accelerate their progression to the Majors.

Thus, the first stop on my quest to the Major Leagues was Pittsfield, Massachusetts. Rooted in western Massachusetts, Pittsfield is the heart of culturally-rich Berkshire County. A small industrial town, Pittsfield was where energy giant General Electric called home during its growth to notoriety. Though not exactly what I considered a tourist city, its scenic landscape captured my heart. Beautiful Lake Onota centered my attraction to Pittsfield's geography. I spent many days down by the lake to pacify my stressful baseball season.

Waconah Park was the home stadium of the Pittsfield Astros. Built primarily to be used for football games, the baseball field at Waconah Park was oddly constructed. The playing surface had dimensions abnormal for baseball. The center field wall was about 500 feet deep, and it got deeper as the wall jutted out in right-center field. On the other hand, the left-field fence was no further than 300 feet. To make matters worse, sometimes the sun would shine directly in the batter's face during games. The intense sunlight shining from left field made it almost impossible for the batter to see the ball when it was pitched. Therefore, games were often postponed until the sun went down. It was the first time I had ever played in a game that was suspended due to sunlight.

Walking into the locker room at Waconah Park for the first time was absolutely shocking. It was unbelievable how small the space was. It appeared like there were more players than there were lockers. All the players were packed into the locker room like a sardine can. While everyone appeared comfortable with their bags unpacked and locker organized, I was trying to find some personal space. Since I joined the team late, due to the College World Series, there was not much visible space left to occupy. I placed my belongings in the corner of the locker room and walked over to the coaches' office. Inside the office, I introduced myself to head coach and former Major League infielder, Ivan DeJesus. Nicknamed "Pulpo," which means octopus in Spanish, DeJesus played over 10 seasons in the Major Leagues. He informed me that I could work out with the team, but I couldn't play in the games yet. I had to sit out for a few days until my contract paperwork was ratified by Major League Baseball.

At first glance, I thought we had a bunch of Black players on our team. But as soon as they spoke, it became obvious to me that they weren't Black. They were Latino players from multiple countries, including the Dominican Republic and Venezuela. I was shocked by how much they looked just like me, with their dark brown skin and curly black hair. Even though they spoke very little English (if any at all), I had an early connection with the Latin players. Most of them had no family in the United States, and therefore had very little knowledge of how to operate here in the states. I always tried to help them do the little things, like shop for groceries or cash a check. Since I was regularly the only Black player on the team, I spent most of time hanging with the Latin players. Ironically, I could relate to them better than many of my teammates that were born in the United States. I later learned how Latin players familiarized themselves with Black people as well. They too acknowledged that we shared some of the same obstacles in life as minorities. I would continue to befriend Latin players throughout my entire baseball career.

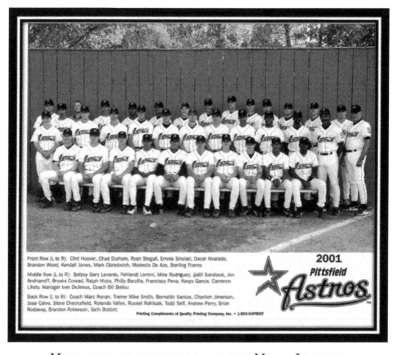

MY FIRST STOP ON THE ROAD TO THE MAJOR LEAGUES

Since I couldn't play yet, I used my time on the bench to meet some of the guys on the team. There was one other Black player on the team besides myself named Cameron Likely. A country boy from Pensacola, Florida, Likely was drafted from of the University of South Alabama in the 24th round. His even-keeled personality made people want to be around him. He always kept a moderate temperament and never let his emotions control his actions. It was nice to have another Black player on the team to hang out with, someone who shared the same cultural interests as myself. Having someone that relates to you—by default—based on racial or ethnical background is a luxury that I believe white baseball players take for granted. The feeling of acceptance by peers is built upon shared interests such as music, movies, and extracurricular activities. These similarities are highly dependent on the demographics of the team, with emphasis on ethnicity.

One thing that made me feel more comfortable in Pittsfield, was knowing that my buddy Mike Rodriguez would be joining me. Mike was also drafted by the Houston Astros in the 2001 MLB Draft. He was selected in the 2nd round, and decided to forego his senior year at Miami to play professional baseball. When Mike Rodriguez arrived, we lived together as roommates along with pitcher Russ Rohlichek. We lived in the home of a host family—a retired couple who was kind enough to open their home for us. They were avid fans of baseball games at Waconah Park. For the 2001 season, they decided to offer cheap housing to a few players. We paid $100 of our $400 bi-weekly paychecks for rent to live at their house. We slept in the downstairs basement of a beautiful two-story home. The basement was surprisingly spacious, with two twin beds and an air mattress for the three of us to sleep on. We weren't required to pay utilities for the house and the refrigerator was open to all. Occasionally, we would come home starving and raid their refrigerator. We received *per diem*, or meal money from the Houston Astros of about $10 to help pay for food. But I realized right away that our paychecks weren't sufficient to cover the cost of living in Pittsfield. The Houston Astros didn't pay us enough every two weeks to cover our day-to-day expenses. Luckily, I had residual money from my signing bonus to help support me financially during the season.

That season, I started in center field almost daily and mostly hit third in the batting order. I really wanted to show the Houston Astros that I could make the transition from college to professional baseball. The first step in my mission was getting used to hitting with wooden bats instead of metal. Since I had only used metal bats in college, hitting with a wood bat was foreign to me. I had to familiarize myself with the size, weight, and barrel of a wood bat. These three components were some of the essential differences between wood and aluminum bats. The barrel and handle of a wood bat have to be balanced. The length and weight must be an ideal combination for the player. If not, the swing does not function properly. It's like a knight trying to swing a sword that is too heavy or too long. I recognized early that I couldn't get away with the things that I used to get away with swinging aluminum bats. In college, balls that I did not hit well would still come off the bat hard with an aluminum bat. With a wood bat, the bat would break almost every time I got jammed inside or hit a ball off the end of the bat. To me, finding a bat that felt comfortable once it was in my hands was most important. It allowed me to focus on hitting the ball and not be distracted by the bat. Granted, selecting the right bat can become a chore with so many models to choose from. After breaking enough bats to make firewood, I found that having the bat personally made to my specifications was best. It allowed me to piece together the components of a wood bat to my liking.

Regrettably, my transition to professional baseball began with embarrassment. My first road game was against the New Jersey Cardinals, a New York Penn League affiliate of the St. Louis Cardinals. After checking into the hotel, we had time to grab some food before our 3 p.m. bus to the stadium. After eating lunch with a couple of my teammates, I went back to my room, while my roommate Mike Rodriguez hung out in the lobby. As our bus time approached, I started to get dressed in my uniform. Back in college, we always dressed in our uniforms at the hotel. Then as a team, we loaded everything on the bus, and went to the stadium. After the game, we would load everything back on the bus, and return in our dirty uniforms. Once we arrived at the hotel, we would shower and change clothes in our rooms. Therefore, with that in mind, I went down to the bus dressed in my Pittsfield Astros uniform. As soon as I set foot on the bus, I realized I was no longer in college. Somehow, I was the last to know that in professional baseball, players dress for the game in the locker room at the stadium. Everyone, including Mike, was crying laughing when I walked on the bus. All my teammates were properly dressed in collared shirts and jeans. I was the only idiot on the bus in my Pittsfield Astros uniform. To make matters worse, I had to wear my dirty uniform back to the hotel. It was a moment I will never forget throughout my baseball career. And a moment that Mike will never let me forget, even if I tried.

At the Rookie level, it seems like all the players care about is what round a player got drafted, and how much money he signed for. Many guys are jealous of how much money someone else received as a signing bonus. Since the Rookie season begins weeks after the MLB draft, many players feel some type of way about their position in the draft. In Pittsfield, several players felt like they deserved to be drafted higher. Others felt like they should have received more money in their contract. Unfortunately, I was the target of some unwarranted jealousy and envy from my teammates. Because of my success in college, other players assumed that I had everything handed to me on a platter. Before they got the chance to know me, they judged me. I never understood why my teammates would be mad at me over the contract I signed. I did not demand to be drafted higher or receive a larger signing bonus. It was the Astros decision to draft me in the 5th round. And it was the Astros who offered to give me a signing bonus. How could anyone be mad at me for what the Houston Astros decided to do? Instead of players hating on me, they should have been mad at the Houston Astros.

Because of the hatred, I had to choose my friends on the team wisely. I wanted to distance myself away from the negativity and simply focus on playing baseball. I've always had a keen sense of reading people, so I was good at detecting which individuals had good intentions. Through it all, I remained confident and never let their negative energy affect my self-esteem. Besides, there was nothing they could say that could break me. I had been through too much in my life to let their harsh words prevent me from excelling.

On the field, I was still learning how to play the game at the professional level. I worked on my swing day after day, trying to become a better hitter. Major League Baseball great Reggie Jackson once told me to "*Hit, hit, hit...then hit again until perfect.*" That's what I planned to do while in Pittsfield. Hitting coach Marc Ronan, and roving hitting instructor Johnny Lewis worked with me constantly in the batting cage. Johnny Lewis (or J-Lew) was a heavyset Black guy, with bulging eyes and a dusty gray beard. His low raspy voice demanded attention without yelling and screaming. Johnny Lewis was a gentle giant, who quickly earned respect and admiration from me and many other players. We were all inspired by the way he challenged guys to hit the ball hard and with a purpose.

Spending time with Johnny Lewis was very special to me and Cameron. He shared stories about the Jim Crow era, when Blacks weren't welcomed in the United States of America. He revealed how Blacks in Major League Baseball were not allowed to stay in the team hotel on road trips. At that time, hotels only accommodated white people. Therefore, Black players made "lemonade out of lemons" and stayed in the Black neighborhoods when playing on the road. The players received home-cooked meals and southern hospitality from the people kind enough to open their homes. Amongst familiar faces, the Black players were celebrities in the Black community. Based on a history of inequality, he warned us to never forget that we were Black in a white man's game. And due to the remaining racial imbalance in baseball, Black players in today's game have to play twice as good to get equal recognition. Those three months, from June 2001 until September 2001, were unforgettable. Playing in Pittsfield was a valuable step in my baseball career. Not only because it helped develop my baseball skills, but it also helped me grow as a man.

In February 2002, I reported to Astros Minor League spring training in Kissimmee, Florida. Spring training for Major League Baseball begins annually in the month of February. This was my first trip to spring training since I started playing my rookie season in June 2001. Everyone—players and coaches—had hyped-up spring training so much during the off-season. They stressed how important it was to show up ready to spring training. So I spent my time before spring training working out in the gym, and building overall strength and flexibility. I did speed training for running explosion, as well as long distance running for endurance. Besides, I needed to prepare for the mile and a half run in 10 minutes and

30 seconds. All the players in Astros Minor League spring training had to complete the run or repeat until completed. Houston sent each player a handbook to help them train for the mile and a half run. The handbook also included suggested weight lifting programs, good eating habits, and multiple stretching techniques. The Astros did a good job of providing the players with information.

When I arrived at spring training, I was alarmed by how many players were in attendance. I didn't realize how many players were members of the Houston Astros organization. Almost every player, even the Major League players, were at spring training. The Minor League players trained on one-half of the facility, and the Major League players occupied the other half of the facility. At times, the Major League players would practice on the baseball field right next to the Minor League players. It was almost as if the Houston Astros staff wanted the Minor League players to see the Major League players. That way, the Minor League players can envision their Major League dream within arm's reach. Since I had only played a short season of rookie ball, there was a multitude of people that I didn't know. Some of the players were friendly and welcomed me to the Astros organization. While some were cold and never spoke a word to me at all. They could care less who I was. Many players were fighting for their careers, because being released could mean it's time to hang up the cleats. There was no time to make friends or build relationships. Besides, I needed to focus on preparing myself for the upcoming 2002 season.

Because this was my first spring training, I didn't want to put too much pressure on myself. I simply wanted to do well and show the Astros staff that I was ready for the next level. Minor League spring training with the Astros was like boot camp. Each day we worked out from roughly 6 a.m. to nearly 5 p.m. We practiced team drills in the mornings, and played games in the afternoon. Minor League spring training games are similar to high school baseball games. The only fans in attendance to watch the games are family and girlfriends. There is nothing glamorous at all about Minor League spring training.

HOUSTON ASTROS SPRING TRAINING IN KISSIMMEE, FLORIDA

At the time, we had two Single-A Low teams, and no Single-A-High team. Almost every other MLB organization had one Single-A Low team, and one Single-A High team. So, I was either going to play in Lexington, Kentucky in the South Atlantic League; or I was going to play in Battle Creek, Michigan in the Midwest League. I desperately wanted to play in Lexington because I hated playing in cold weather, and I heard teams in Michigan sometimes played baseball games in snowy weather. Lexington also had a manager who I wanted to play for. Joseph Jerome (or J.J.) Cannon had a favorable reputation amongst the players he coached. I was highly interested in playing for a Black manager, which was something I had never experienced before.

After days of seeing players either switch team rosters or released, the season rosters for each level were finalized. Luckily, I was on the Lexington Legends' team roster, while most of my ex-teammates from Pittsfield were on the Michigan Battlecats' team roster. One of those ex-teammates not joining me in Lexington was Mike Rodriguez. Although I was excited about playing in Kentucky, I was disappointed that my *roomie* would not be going with me. Mike was slated to play for the Michigan Battlecats. For the first time since winning two National Championships at Miami, Mike and I would be on different teams.

After our final workout in spring training, I drove my newly purchased 2001 Chevy Tahoe for nearly thirteen hours straight to Lexington, Kentucky. Good thing I had driving directions because I had no clue where Kentucky was. All I knew was that the people there loved horse racing and something about the grass being blue. When I arrived in Lexington, it looked just like any other major city I had visited. Only Lexington had one of the cleanest, yet most developed downtown areas I had ever seen. Most of our team was encouraged to stay at the Grand Reserve apartments, an upscale apartment complex located just twenty minutes from the stadium. Like most of my teammates, I also decided to rent an apartment there. While at the leasing office, I befriended Brandon Caraway, an outfielder from Texas who previously played in the Philadelphia Phillies organization. We connected almost immediately, mostly because Caraway enjoyed Black culture. He was the epitome of what we call "White Chocolate" in the Black community. He listened to hip-hop music, loved southern-cooked meals, and had swag. Days later, Caraway and I became roommates when we moved into a two-bedroom apartment together.

The day before the season began, we had a team meeting. J.J. Cannon and his staff introduced themselves to the players and went over team rules. I think I stared at J.J. throughout the entire meeting, trying to read his body language. I had never had a Black baseball coach before. Shit, I barely had Black teammates on previous teams and there certainly weren't any on the 2002 Lexington Legends roster. I was trying to determine how I should conduct myself around J.J. I could already sense that he would demand a certain formality and discipline maintained between him and all his players. I didn't feel that any preferential treatment would be given to me because we were both Black.

Before long, J.J. and I built a close relationship that was more than just player and coach. He became somewhat of a father figure to me through the many talks we had about life and baseball. J.J. played in the Major Leagues for the Houston Astros and the Toronto Blue Jays. It was now his job as a coach to teach me the principals I needed to know to help me to get there. I started the season out hot, absolutely on fire. In the first month of April, I hit an eye popping .340. I was smashing home runs on offense, and catching everything in sight on defense. For my performance, I was named both the team's offensive and defensive player of the month in April. These awards were highly respected within the Houston Astros organization. I was extremely proud to be selected to receive these prestigious awards.

Judging by the way that I played in the first month, I pretty much thought the season was going to be a cake walk. However, it wouldn't be long before I reached my peak and went stumbling downhill. Though my defense remained strong, the months of June and July were rough offensively. My batting average dropped dramatically and the strikeouts piled up. I didn't know how to change my repeated disappointing results. I knew I needed to adjust my approach to hitting, but I was too immature in my baseball development to make the correct adjustment. Therefore, my struggles lasted months in time, instead of weeks or days.

Despite my steady decline in performance, I was nominated to the 2002 South Atlantic League All-Star Game in Lakewood, New Jersey. It was the first all-star game I played in since my Little League days, so I was honored and extremely excited to be there. The game was filled with big time prospects from other MLB organizations like Ryan Howard and Justin Huber. Coming off the bench for the Southern Division, I went 1-for-2 with a double, and a run scored to help our team win the game 2-1. Being a participant in the South Atlantic All-Star Game was one of the most gratifying moments in my entire baseball career.

Unfortunately, the fun didn't last very long because right after the all-star break, I returned to playing awful. Applebee's Park, our home stadium, had a left field wall that was very short in distance. Game after game I tried so hard to hit the ball as far as I could over that left field wall. It was a constant internal battle to swallow my pride and just try to make contact with the ball. If I just focused on hitting the ball with solid contact, and not smashing home runs, I would have had better success at the plate.

I finished the year hitting a miserable .228 with 168 strikeouts. Although I struggled throughout the season, being around some of the veteran players on the team made it easier to bear. One player in particular continuously helped me to stay focused mentally. Brian Schmitt, a first baseman from Texas, was kind enough to share his wisdom with me. He reminded me daily of the bigger picture, which was to gain experience to help me develop into a Major League baseball player. He encourage me to forget about all the swinging and missing I had done, and focus on what was to be learned from each strikeout. I really enjoyed his presence on the team and the leadership qualities he possessed.

Playing my first full season of professional baseball not only took its toll on me mentally, but physically as well. The travel was hardest on my body. Sometimes we rode twelve to fourteen hours each way on a charter bus to play teams. For those trips, many guys bought egg crate mattress pads to put on the bus floor underneath the seats. When a player wanted to sleep, they crawled down on the floor and laid down on the mattress pad. This was the only hope of getting somewhat of a decent night's sleep while on the bus. It was next to impossible for me to feel physically able to play well after sleeping on the bus. My body always felt tight, thus making my swing feel forced instead of fluid. The first game after arriving at the stadium was guaranteed my worse offensive performance of the road series.

Overall, I learned a lot during my season in Lexington. Most importantly, I learned how to maintain my health and fitness. Working out, getting a good night's sleep, and eating a healthy breakfast were all key factors for me to play my best baseball. Many nights I would go out in downtown Lexington and party with the students from the University of Kentucky. I routinely partied until 2 a.m., before eating fast food and passing out drunk at my apartment. I guess I thought I could go out drinking and partying at clubs as if I was still in college. The difference was, I had a job to perform each night. And almost every night

I went out and partied, I played a horrible game the following day. I would never understand the consequences of my partying habits until after I retired. My infatuation with women, alcohol, and nightclubs continued to hinder my performance on the field throughout my entire baseball career.

Playing in Lexington taught me how to balance both my personal life and baseball career. During the six-month season, I learned to take responsibility for my actions. For example, if I was late arriving to the stadium, I had to report directly to J.J. Cannon and explain my tardiness. However he chose to discipline me for my actions, I had to accept it and move forward. In short, I had to learn how to be a professional. The foundation of the development of a Minor League player into a Major League Baseball player is the individual's understanding of how to be a professional.

7th Inning:

After experiencing another challenging and exhausting spring training in Kissimmee, I began my second full season of baseball in Salem, Virginia. The Salem Avalanche were the new Carolina League Single-A High affiliate of the Houston Astros in 2003. Located about thirty miles outside of Roanoke, Salem is nestled between the Allegany and the Blue Ridge Mountains. Because of these geographical elements, the town always had a forecast of overcast skies, and intermittent rain. Sometimes, Salem had a gloomy mist that reflected that of a horror movie scene.

At that time, not having no Single-A High level established for Astros prospects was a deficiency in the Houston Astros' player development. In the past, players in the organization would have to advance from Single-A Low, directly to the Double-A level. But many players struggled with the transition from Single-A Low to Double-A. The Single-A High level was designed to give players extra time to develop their skills before competing at the Double-A level. Houston now had a Single-A High team intact to allow players that time to develop.

The Salem Avalanche were managed by John Massarelli, who was promoted from Single-A Low, where he managed the Michigan Battlecats in 2002. During spring training, I heard that Massarelli was the type of manager who really wanted to win. Former players informed me that if a player didn't perform well, he wouldn't speak to that player while he struggled. And if the team struggled collectively, he would show his displeasure through his toddler-like tantrums. With that said, I wasn't the least bit excited to play for Massarelli.

However, if playing for Massarelli was what I needed to do for me to advance, then I was prepared to do it. My focus was set on improving my baseball skills and competing at the next level. Rounding out the staff were pitching coach, Stan Boroski, and hitting coach, Pete Rancont.

The weather in sunny California and steamy Florida were polar opposites to the frigid state of Virginia. The forecast in Salem was always cold and rainy, with a chance of snowfall. I was not happy about playing baseball in the cold and rain. At least, I had my buddy Mike Rodriguez back as a teammate to help me stay positive in the miserable weather conditions. Mike's experience from playing baseball in cold weather in Michigan allowed him to share some tips on how to conquer the cold. Unlike in Lexington, I didn't burst out of the gate like a horse at the Kentucky Derby. I began the season just like the daily weather forecast—cold. However, I was mentally content with my slow start. My goal was to continue to improve throughout the season. But constant rain delays and canceled games made it hard to remain consistent. Whenever I felt good at the plate for a couple of games, the next game would be rained out. Even when my swing felt good during a game, it would rain and we'd have a three-hour rain delay. When a player is hitting good, the last thing he wants is break from the game. The only good thing about all the rain delays was the extra time we spent together as a team. During a rain delay, we all huddled in the clubhouse to wait out the storm. In the clubhouse, we shared stories, played card games, and watched television for hours. The camaraderie we built off the field, carried over onto the field during the games. Spending time together was important to our team's success. It's an intangible advantage on the field when a team likes one another, and spends quality time together off the field. We won a lot more games than we should have based on our desire to play for one another.

About midway through the season, I started getting hot at the plate. My batting average rose, and I began to show hitting power to all parts of field. It didn't matter whether I was playing at home, or on the road, I was on fire. And my hits were not just singles—they were doubles, triples, and home runs—in bunches. Unfortunately, right after heating up, my hand was broken by a pitch during a game in Frederick, Maryland. In my first two at-bats of the game against the Frederick Keys, I homered and doubled off the wall. But in my third at-bat, I was intentionally hit in the left hand by a pitch. Often times, pitchers will intentionally hit batters with a pitch when they can't get the batter out. It's a typical cowardly move by pitchers who can't get a guy out with strikes. The ball was thrown towards my face at nearly 90 mph, so I moved my hands off the bat to protect myself. Instead of the ball smashing into my face, it plunked me in the back of my hand. I heard something pop, and immediately felt the pain erupting from my left hand. The first thought in my mind was that my hand was broken, and I would be out for the remainder of the season. Luckily, after a visit to a local hospital, X-rays revealed that it was just a hairline fracture in my hand. The injury would only put me out for about six weeks. My hand was in a splint for about a month. I was pissed off that my season was interrupted by the injury. But I remained focused on the ultimate goal of making it to the Major Leagues. I knew I would be back playing again in due time.

It was tough to sit on the bench and watch game after game, with no chance of playing. I ate sunflower seeds and chewed bubble gum…ate some more seeds, and chewed more gum. I was miserable from the inability to play. I felt useless having to sit and watch while my teammates battle on the baseball field. During that time, I suffered from depression. I was taking prescription pain medication while drinking alcohol on a nightly basis. I even started smoking cigarettes after games at night. My roommate Mike Rodriguez would support me through the rough times. His companionship carried me through this emotionally challenging period in my life. Sometimes, even the toughest of athletes need someone to talk to that will simply listen without passing judgment. Mike was that person for me. When I got older, I realized that men do not openly talk about being depressed for fear of being viewed as less masculine. But like a deadly gas leak, depression can seep into a man's life without notice. And one day, the simplest of events could cause the spark that creates a life-threatening explosion. Feelings and emotions are human nature, so if you don't have an outlet for these emotions, you are putting your health at-risk. It was vital to my health to stop feeling sorry for myself and get back on the field and do what I enjoyed doing—giving people hell on the baseball field.

HURRICANE WARNING IN

UNIVERSITY OF MIAMI DUO SPARKS AVALANCHE

BY GENE MARRANO

They hail from different coasts. One grew up as an only child in a traditional family with a mother and father around; the other has four siblings and was raised largely by an older sister after both his parents had "issues" dealing with drug and physical abuse. But Salem Avalanche outfielders **Mike Rodriguez** and **Charlton Jimerson** bonded during their time together at the University of Miami — where they won two national NCAA championships and have been close ever since.

Rodriguez, 22, was selected by the Astros in the second round of the 2001 draft and Jimerson, 23, was picked up by Houston three rounds later. They went in tandem to Pittsfield, Mass., for short-season rookie ball before splitting up for the first time in more than four years during the 2002 season, when both were all-stars. Jimerson — his first name Charlton was inspired in part by his mother **Charlene** and in part by actor **Charlton Heston** — hit just .228 for the low-A Michigan Battle Cats under current Avs' manager **John Massarelli**. "CJ," as Rodriguez calls him, did pound out 14 home runs and 57 runs batted in while stealing 34 bases. Meanwhile "M-Rod" swiped

Charlton Jimerson (left) and Mike Rodriguez won two College World Series at Miami. They hope to win another title with the Avalanche.

where the Avalanche has put him.   kind of stupid for a guy to get rid

HURRICANE WARNING: ME AND MY ROOMIE MIKE RODRIGUEZ

I knew I could help my team win, so I was prepared to do whatever to get back to playing ball. In order to get back on the field, I needed get healthy and strengthen my hand. Once the splint was removed, I began physical rehabilitation for my hand. Rehabilitation for my hand required numerous hand strengthening exercises. I used hand weights, handgrips, and even a bucket of rice to increase my hand strength. I would stick my hand in a bucket of rice—grab a hand full of rice—and release. I would repeat this exercise about 30 times, or until my hand became fatigued. Each rehabilitation session concluded with icing my hand to prevent any further swelling. I was working hard every day to get off the bench and back on the field.

Returning to playing form in 2003 was of greater importance because it was my protection year. That meant that at the end of the season, I could be added to the 40-man Major League roster. Being added to the roster would put me one step closer to Houston. Players on the 40-man roster are invited to participate in Major League spring training instead of Minor League spring training. Once a player is competing in Major League spring training, there is always a chance of making the team in Houston. Therefore, I really wanted to have a productive season. I worried that my injury would rob me of valuable take playing time that I could never get back.

Unlike several other players during that era, I didn't consider using steroids or human growth hormone to recover from injury. At that time, many baseball players were using performing-enhancing drugs (PEDs) to speed up their recovery or enhance their overall performance. These drugs can reduce recovery time, increase physical strength, or prevent fatigue over the course of a baseball season. Performance-enhancing drugs would later be banned from use in Major League Baseball, but at that time, using PEDs were not illegal. This period in baseball would later be tabbed as the "Steroid Era." It was not until after my career ended that I reflected on how difficult it was to compete during the Steroid Era. When some players are using PEDs to enhance their performance on the field, the players who aren't using PEDs are at a competitive disadvantage. I was one of those players who respected the integrity of the game of baseball and never used a banned substance. However, players who took PEDs and perform well on the field because of it, were rewarded with lucrative MLB contracts. It was hypocritical by nature for Major League Baseball to inform players about the risks of using PEDs, impose penalties for players who tested positive for PEDs, but yet reward those same players with hefty contracts in the future. Making it to the Major Leagues during The Steroid Era was a tall task for any player who opted not to use performance-enhancing drugs. My odds of making it to the Major Leagues decreased significantly because the number of players using PEDs to improve their performance increased dramatically.

Surprisingly, my injury allowed me to mental break from all the pressure of playing professional baseball. From my new position on the bench, I could see the game from a coach's perspective. My vantage point allowed me to learn from the game while being inactive. I was able to observe how other players reacted to different situations in the game. At that time, I learned more from watching their mistakes than actually playing. It was sort of like college revisited because I was sitting on the bench game after game. Only this time I was on the bench due to injury, and not because the coaches felt I wasn't worthy of playing.

When I returned from my injury, I felt weird being back on the field. My hiatus from playing baseball made something that was so natural to me, feel foreign. An injury can take a player out of their comfort zone. A player that once ran fast or jumped high prior to injury, wonders if they will be able to do the same when they are back healthy. I was unsure of how I would hit after returning to the lineup. Even though I was healthy, I did not feel the same strength and power I displayed before my injury. The bat felt different in my hands, and I was constantly nervous that I would feel pain again when swinging. My vision was also skewed when I returned. Pitchers seemed like they were throwing every pitch a 100 miles per hour. It was as if I was starting all over again, learning how to hit for the first time. I had only been out of the game for six weeks, but it felt like an eternity. Being patient with myself would be the key to my progression. I could not expect to return to the lineup hitting doubles and home runs every game. A slow, yet steady progression was the focus of my return. Of course, getting hits always helps with that progression.

Following a night game in Myrtle Beach, South Carolina, hitting coach Pete Rancont came by my locker to speak to me. He asked me to meet him at the field early the next day. I was both a little shocked and nervous about our upcoming meeting. Believe me, no player wants to meet with any coach one-on-one. Especially a meeting with an unknown agenda. The following day, we met at the stadium about 2 p.m. We walked out of the locker room, and onto field, and stood by the left field foul line. As Pete began to talk, he took off his ever-present Oakley sunglasses. He then began expressing to me that there were times when I had chances to hit batting practice early and chose not to. Though it wasn't mandatory, he believed that if I wanted to get better, I needed to start showing up early and putting in the extra work. He stressed to me that many players in the past never advanced past the Carolina League, and I was on my way to being one of those players. If I wanted to advance to Triple-A, I needed to put in the necessary work to elevate my game. Looking back, I now realize that Pete Rancont saved my career on that summer day in Myrtle Beach. He was the only one who cared enough to talk to me honestly, without reserve. The conversation we had truly touched me because it was sincere and straightforward. He didn't have to extend himself to me and challenge me to do better. But he did, and he would have done the same for any player no matter their draft status.

From that day forward, I was back on my grind. I went to the cage every day before games and hit a ton of balls off the batting tee. After tee work, Pete would toss me balls from behind a batting screen. After toss, he would pitch to me for batting practice. In less than two weeks, I was swinging the bat better than I did before my injury. I was hitting balls hard everywhere, even when I made an out. For a long stretch of games, I was in what baseball players call "The Zone." No matter what the pitcher threw me, I crushed it. My play earned me Carolina League Player of the Week honors after batting over .400 during a week in August. I turned my whole season around by hitting nearly .330 for the reminder of the season, and .265 overall. My desire and dedication to my job was tested that season, and I prevailed.

Playing the game itself was hard enough, but dealing with Massarelli made it harder. Towards the end of the season, the Massarelli that players had fore-warned me about began to show. Each mental or physical mistake I made in a game was highlighted and criticized by Massarelli. Not only did he bring those mistakes to my attention, but he also broadcasted them to everyone during team meetings. His condescending tone and offensive behavior caused conflict between us; which almost boiled over into a physical altercation. Looking back on it now, I realize that Massarelli and I just had conflicting personalities. He had what I perceived as an invasive personality, and I was extremely self-protective.

For the first time in my life, I had to do what many working Americans do every day—work at a job where they don't get along with their boss. Most people don't consider playing baseball for a living a job since we play a game for money. But at that time, I felt just like any person who works for a boss that they dislike. I had to humble myself in the workplace because I needed my job and the salary it paid. Ultimately, it was my choice to do what the Houston Astros organization paid me to do. So I moved forward with my job, and finished the season strong.

After the 2003 season, I received a call from Houston Astros General Manager, Tim Purpura. Mr. Purpura congratulated me on a strong finish to my season after returning from injury. He said that I should be proud of my progress since being drafted in 2001. It was pleasing to hear the general manager of the Houston Astros commending me on my performance thus far. Without further hesitation, Mr. Purpura informed me that the Houston Astros planned to add me to the 40-man roster. It was like music to my ears. Being added to the 40-man roster meant everything to me. I worked really hard during the season to attain my goals. Before ending our conversation, Mr. Purpura congratulated me again on a great season. He also said that he looked forward to seeing me in Major League spring training. I was elated when I hung up the phone. It felt like I had just been told that I'd won the lottery. I was excited with anticipation about sharing a locker room with Houston Astros superstars like Jeff Bagwell, Lance Berkman, and Craig Biggio. It was the perfect ending to the 2003 season. I was eager to play baseball again in 2004.

I rode that wave of excitement throughout the entire off-season. It propelled me to lift weights harder, run sprints faster, and take batting practice longer to prepare for the season. I knew that I was now in a position to solidify myself as a Major League prospect. But I also understood that so many other players had been in my exact position, and never made it to the Major Leagues. The odds of a player reaching the Major Leagues are extremely low. The numbers dramatically decreased due rise of international players in Major League Baseball. I realized that if I wanted to take advantage of my opportunity, I needed to be prepared for the upcoming season.

8TH INNING:

Still excited about attending my first Major League camp, I arrived at spring training in Kissimmee, Florida looking sharp. Dress to impress, I wore slacks, a collared shirt, necktie, and dress shoes. I wanted to make an impression on the organization by displaying a professional appearance. Mostly, I think it gave veteran players like Brad Ausmus and Brad Lidge a good laugh. But the laughter helped break the ice with many of the veteran players. My attire opened the door for players to give me some playful advice about both fashion and baseball. They advised me to stay quiet and to try to be seen but not heard. They sternly suggested that I let the veteran players get their work in first and to stay out of their way. Most importantly, they said to play hard and hustle every day. Even though I really wanted to get some autographs and pester them with a million questions, I remained quiet and reserved. I only engaged in conversation with veteran players when they spoke to me first. I needed them to know I respected their seniority. Since this was my first Major League spring training, I sought to ensure I was doing all the right things.

I worked hard every day, hustling in practice during our team drills. Eventually my work ethic caught the attention of Houston Astros manager, Jimy Williams. Williams was starting his third year with the Astros since becoming manager before the 2002 season. A man of few words, Jimy Williams took it upon himself to work with me in the outfield every morning. We usually worked on throwing mechanics, since he stressed the importance of outfielders throwing with the correct form. I appreciated the time he spent with me because it gave me a sense of belonging. I felt like he treated me with the same respect and value as the established Major League players.

During spring training games, I spent most of the time sitting on the bench and observing. As a rookie, I didn't get much playing time. Sometimes I entered games during the late innings, but playing was not guaranteed. I had a better chance of playing during road games, because the veteran players usually opted to not travel on long distance bus trips. After spending two weeks with the Big Leaguers, I was sent down to Minor League spring training. With no real chance of making the Houston Astros team, I mostly benefited from the instruction provided by the Major League coaching staff.

Despite already knowing that I wasn't going to the make the Houston Astros roster, it sucked going back to Minor League camp. Being "sent down" meant packing up my belongings and moving them to the adjacent Minor League facility. It was hard to remain excited about spring training after being sent down to Minor League camp. In Major League spring training we ate catered food, and played games in front of large crowds of baseball fanatics. On the other hand, in Minor League spring training, we ate cafeteria food and played games in front of our family and friends. I could still hear the excitement from the Major League games while I played on the nearby Minor League fields. But, my position in Minor League camp was something I couldn't change. Making sure I played to the best of my ability every time I stepped on the field was the only thing I could control. It was important for me to focus on things I could control. The next stop on my quest to the Major Leagues was Double-A baseball.

The Round Rock Express were the Houston Astros Double-A team in 2004. Mostly all the players who played for the Express spoke highly of the city of Round Rock, Texas. They raved about the state-of-the-art Dell Diamond stadium and the boisterous baseball fans that attended each home game. Reid and Reese Ryan, sons of Hall of Fame pitcher Nolan Ryan, were the owners of the Express. The Ryan brothers were directly responsible for the first class treatment of Express players. As young entrepreneurs who loved the game of baseball, they knew how to balance both business and baseball. Nolan Ryan was often seen checking out a game at Dell Diamond. And it was not uncommon to see actor Matthew McConaughey or cyclist Lance Armstrong in the crowd either. The Express were managed by Jackie Moore, an old soul who coached professional baseball at all levels for many years. Jackie even managed my hometown Oakland Athletics from 1984-1986. He knew the game of baseball, and always forewarned us that "the game will go on without you." The pitching coach was Joe Slusarski and Sean Berry was in charge of hitting. Also joining the staff was former Major League infielder Spike Owen. I'd heard nothing but good things about the entire Round Rock coaching staff and front office personnel.

Another amenity while playing in Round Rock was the "passing of the hat." If an Express player hit a home run during a home game, fans would pass a hat around the crowd and collect money. The money collected was split into three portions—money for the player, money for the team, and money to be donated to a local organization. The extra money the player earned was in addition to his salary. Since I was a power hitter, hitting home runs at Dell Diamond meant more money in my pocket. The fans in Round Rock did things like this just because they loved to see exciting baseball. My anticipation of playing in Round Rock was overwhelming. On the same afternoon that spring training ended, I packed up my Chevy Tahoe and headed for Texas. I drove up the beautiful Atlantic Coast on Interstate 95, to the Florida panhandle. Once I reached Interstate 10, I merged on to I-10 West, and headed towards Mobile, Alabama. Without stopping, I drove past the casinos in Biloxi, Mississippi and kept trucking towards Louisiana. While in the Louisiana, I had to stop in New Orleans to taste Louisiana's world-renowned Cajun-style food. My teammates who were caravanning behind me also stopped to eat lunch in "NOLA." We took a lunch break for about an hour, then resumed driving towards Texas. I was all too familiar with hitting the highway for a fifteen hour drive. With good music to listen to and something to snack on, I could drive for hours. When I arrived in Round Rock, the scenery impressed me. Round Rock had a perfect balance of beautiful landscape and commercial buildings along Interstate 35. The business district was ever-present without sacrificing space for beautiful parks and open ranges. There was a selection of upscale restaurants and nice hotels as well. The city had numerous neighborhood housing communities full of middle-to-upper class families. Round Rock was the perfect place to raise a family.

The 2004 Round Rock Express had a phenomenal group of talented players. Veteran players Dax Norris and Kevin Orie led our team on the field. Rookies Hector Gimenez and Phillip Barzilla provided a surprising boost to our offense and bullpen. Willy Taveras and Luke Scott were newly-acquired outfielders who quickly made an impact. Todd Self, Brooks Conrad, and Jared Gothreaux were also key players who paced our team's success. We had the best defensive outfield any coach could ask for. Mike Rodriguez played in left field, Willy Taveras roamed center field, and I covered right field. Between the three of us, we caught almost everything hit to the outfield. We were a dangerous trio on the base paths too, stealing more than 100 bases between the three of us.

Since our season began on the road, I had time to find housing in Round Rock before our first home stand. Therefore, I stayed in a hotel for the first three days while we practiced and played exhibition games. We played back-to-back days of exhibition games against the New Orleans Zephyrs, the Triple-A affiliate of the Houston Astros. Once the exhibition games concluded, our season commenced in El Paso, Texas. We flew to El Paso on Southwest Airlines the morning of opening day. Travel by airplane was one of the perks of playing Double-A baseball. For years, I had endured long bus rides, so I was excited to board a plane for a change. Any seat on a Southwest Airlines flight was far more comfortable than the egg crate on the bus floor. We opened the season with a six-game series against the El Paso Diablos. The Diablos were the Double-A affiliate of the Arizona Diamondbacks in 2004. We lost our first two games, before winning the next four in a row, to put our record at 4-2. Although I played well in our opening series against the Diablos, I couldn't wait to get home and play at Dell Diamond. I was eager to put on a show for the fans in Round Rock and win them over. Looking back at it now, I was far too anxious. My mind was set on doing much more than what was expected of me. I had no idea that I was headed towards misery and headache after leaving El Paso.

My first few games in Round Rock were terrible. I was dismayed by my awful performance in front of the home crowd. It was the exact opposite of what I had hoped would have transpired. I had a dreadful series and would continue to struggle in home games all season long. I struck out far too often, especially when the situation of the game called for me to just make contact. Just like in Lexington, there was a home run porch in left field that kept calling my name every at-bat. I thought I had learned my lesson, but night after night I continued to strikeout because I was swinging for the fence. I averaged a strikeout a game, sometimes striking out three, four, or five times a game. The frustration was extremely hard to deal with. Unfortunately, I let my offensive struggles affect my play on defense. I was so mentally defeated that I couldn't separate the offensive and defensive aspects of the game. I desperately needed to make an adjustment and get back to playing baseball the way I was capable of playing.

Before each game, I continued to hit in the batting cages with Sean Berry. Each day I hoped that I had made the necessary change in my swing to fix all my problems. But, the changes I made with my swing only provided temporary success before I returned to looking defeated at the plate. Some games, I would hit balls so hard that it sounded like gunshots firing. And other games, I would swing and miss again like I was a blind man. I looked so bad, that some coaches even suggested that I get my vision checked. I was a "streaky hitter," so when I struggled, I struggled terribly. It was strikeout after strikeout, sometimes six or seven strikeouts in a row. And when it was going well, it was unbelievable to watch some of the balls I hit. What some call streaky hitting, others view as inconsistent. In baseball, not being able to avoid extensive hitting slumps is most often considered as inconsistent. Whatever it was, it was definitely frustrating. Even though I was far more talented than the most of my competition, my weaknesses had been exposed. My inability to adjust hampered my natural ability to compete.

Competition is defined as a rivalry for supremacy or a prize. In the game of baseball, the competition is constantly changing. Sometimes the prize is getting a hit during a game. Other times, the prize is simply not allowing your competitor to continue to beat you in the same manner. I was striking out game after game by swinging at the same bad pitches. Making adjustments every day is the key to longevity in the sport of baseball. Double-A baseball is the tipping point for Minor League players. Once a player reaches Double-A, it's time to go hard or go home. Every player thinks they're ready to play at that level, but only the best can hold their own against other future Major Leaguers. It's a level that weeds out those who can't compete at the highest level, from those who can. Many Major League Baseball organizations believe that playing in Triple-A is not a necessary requirement for a Major League player. Most will not hesitate to move a player to the Major Leagues directly from Double-A. I knew that I desperately needed to improve my hitting if I wanted to advance pass Double-A. My dream of making it to the Major Leagues would be stopped short if I didn't make some adjustments.

I never committed to adjusting my focus, therefore I continued to struggle in Double-A. In the Texas League, teams played each other over twenty-five times a season. Once a team found a weakness in an opposing player, they attempted to expose it every chance they got. Opposing pitchers had figured out the flaws in my swing, and attacked it every at-bat. The Express coaching staff continually tried to help me stay mentally focused throughout my struggles. Jackie suggested that I focus on what is to be learned from each at-bat. Despite the outcome, he understood that there was knowledge to be gained from each at-bat. For example, if I struck out swinging at a curveball. I should log in my memory the location, velocity, and break of the curveball. That way, I could use that information to my benefit for future at-bats. Sometimes in baseball, it's as simple as gathering more information to be successful. Pitching coach Jim Slusarski believed that maybe I set my expectations too high. He suggested that instead getting so frustrated at myself, be patient and understand that I was playing against tough competition. He wanted me to recognize that with so many games against the same team, it's tough for every player to adjust in the Texas League. Pitchers are trying to adjust to hitters, and vice versa. Therefore I wasn't alone in my struggles. I just needed to concentrate on steady progression, and not on immediate results. I still had over 100 games left to play, which would provide plenty of opportunities to succeed.

Our season success allowed us to advance directly to the Texas League championship. By rule, winning both the first and second halves of the regular season gave us a first round bye in the playoffs. Standing in our way of a championship was the Frisco Roughriders, the 2004 Double-A affiliate of the Texas Rangers. Though I was excited about the opportunity to win another championship ring, I was equally excited that my season statistics would no longer matter. In the playoffs, players get a "clean state" to start the post-season. Whatever transpired over the course of the regular season had little significance. All that mattered now was who would play the better in the playoffs.

Two games before the conclusion of the regular season, Willy Taveras was called up to the Houston Astros. Willy was a prime example of a player going directly from Double-A to the Major Leagues. Willy was our leadoff hitter all year long, while I usually hit sixth or seventh in the batting order. With Willy now gone, I assumed I would be our leadoff hitter for the playoffs. To my surprise, Jackie Moore put me eighth in the batting order. I had not hit eighth all season long, so I was highly upset. I knew I was more beneficial to the team batting first in the order than eighth. In the eighth spot, the pitcher always batted behind me in the ninth spot. This caused me to be extremely limited offensively. Opposing pitchers didn't have to pitch to me if they didn't want to. All they had to do was throw pitches out of the strike zone and hope that I would swing. If I didn't swing, and walked instead, the next batter up was the pitcher. And typically, the pitcher is not an offensive threat.

With that batting order in place, we inevitably lost the 2004 Texas League championship to the Frisco Roughriders. Although I had an incredible series at the plate, we struggled as a team offensively. Despite being the hottest hitter on the team throughout the playoffs, Jackie never moved me up in the line-up. Therefore, my personal success didn't breed team success because my hits didn't do much damage from the eight spot. When I hit a double or home run, nobody was on base to score. When I was on base, I rarely scored because the pitcher was a sure out behind me. It was sad to see our once dominant team, be dominated in the playoffs. With a different batting order, we could have easily captured a Texas League championship.

I was hurt because I thought Jackie and I had a pretty good player-coach relationship. Throughout the year, we had so many conversations about staying positive and believing in myself. But during the most critical part of the year, Jackie didn't believe in me. I learned my lesson the hard way. No matter how good the relationship between a player and coach, the coach still has to make decisions based on his own understanding. Baseball managers depend on statistics and scouting reports to make their decisions, more than their personal intuition. Unfortunately, Jackie missed the mark bad when summing up what I could bring to the table in the playoffs, and it probably cost us a championship ring.

A few days after the playoffs ended, I settled down for the off-season. I was really looking forward to a break from baseball after such a mentally challenging year. In baseball, a hitter must be able to accept and refuse failure at the same time. For example, a player is considered great if they can continually get three hits every ten at-bats (30%). With that said, that same player is unsuccessful the other remaining seven at-bats (70%). Therefore, the player can choose to either focus on the three successful hits, or the seven failed attempts. A hitter must be able to accept his failures as a part of the game, yet deny the presence of failure at the same time. It took me a long time to find a comfortable balance of success and failure.

I learned an important life lesson from my experience in Round Rock. If I was going to be my biggest critic, I also needed to be my biggest cheerleader. If I got down on myself for my mistakes, then I needed to congratulate myself for my achievements. Since I couldn't rely on anyone else to believe in me, I needed to be my own one-man fan club. From that day forward, I became a big fan of Charlton Jimerson and dedicated my love and attention to myself.

For whatever reason, the 2005 season seemed to arrive a bit faster than usual. Maybe, it was because my off season was spent playing more baseball in the Arizona Fall League. The Arizona Fall League is a Major League Baseball affiliated league which takes place annually in the fall in Arizona.

The league is comprised of the top Minor League prospects from each Major League organization. There are approximately six Arizona Fall League teams that play games at several Major League Baseball spring training facilities in the Phoenix area. The Houston Astros wanted me to continue to develop while playing for the Scottsdale Scorpions. The Scorpions consisted of players from six different MLB organizations, including the Houston Astros. Players such as James Loney (Los Angeles Dodgers), Dustin Mosely (Cincinnati Reds), Dustin Pedroia (Boston Red Sox), Connor Jackson (Arizona Diamondbacks), and Anthony Gwynn Jr. (Milwaukee Brewers) all played for the Scorpions in 2004.

Playing in the Arizona Fall League was an unbelievable experience. Some of my fondest memories of playing professional baseball took place in the dessert heat of Phoenix, Arizona and its surrounding areas. League games were mostly played at 1 p.m., which usually meant scorching hot weather conditions. However, every Sunday was an off-day which allowed us to take a break from the heat. Although I hated playing so many day games, I enjoyed the free time in the evenings. Just like with anything in life, there were risks and rewards to playing day games and having Sundays off. More free time at night, meant more time to party in Arizona. And just about every player in the Arizona Fall League took advantage of the party scene in Scottsdale, Arizona.

One Sunday afternoon, a bunch of the players in the Arizona Fall League went to watch the Arizona Cardinals football game. The Cardinals were facing the Seattle Seahawks, whom just acquired Hall of Fame wide receiver Jerry Rice. I went to the game with teammates Connor Jackson and Kevin Howard. Kevin was also my teammate at the University of Miami. Connor and Kevin grew up near each other in Thousand Oaks, California. Just like many other professional baseball players, they both enjoyed the herbal pleasure of smoking marijuana. On our way to the game, Connor and Kevin started rolling up their marijuana in the car. Once it was perfectly rolled, they took turns smoking. I paid them no mind because like I mentioned before, marijuana usage is common amongst baseball players. All of sudden, Connor turned around and attempted to pass me the joint. Although I'd smoked marijuana before, it wasn't my drug of choice. I'll happily take a Crown and Coke over smoking weed any day of the week. But that day, I succumbed to peer pressure and inhaled several hits. Within minutes, Connor's Cadillac Escalade truck was filled with marijuana smoke. We continued to take turns smoking, so I was already high by the time we arrived at Sun Devil Stadium. We parked at the stadium and proceeded to the gate entrances.

Sometime during the course of us entering the stadium and finding our seats, my marijuana high intensified. The hot dessert temperature increased the effects the marijuana had on my body. While walking through the concourse, I felt like everything was moving in slow motion. I navigated through the crowds of people holding hot dogs, nachos and fountain drinks. It was like a scene from The Matrix trilogy. My feelings of awareness intensified threefold, eventually causing paranoia to seep in. Once we met up with the other players on the team, I felt awkward and didn't want to talk to anyone. I didn't want them to recognize just how high I actually was. I was paranoid, so whenever someone asked me a question, I replied in a whispering tone. I was too high to gauge how loud my voice was! I could tell everyone was wondering what was wrong with me (or maybe I was just high). Several guys began laughing and antagonizing me by continuously asking me questions. All of sudden, I heard the little voice of my subconscious telling me to leave the stadium. So I whispered (of course) to Connor that I needed to go back to the car. He laughed and handed me the keys. While others conversed, I slipped away from the group without notice. Within minutes, I was back in the comfort of Connor's Escalade truck. I turned on the car so the A/C could cool me down from the Arizona heat. Connor's truck had a mobile TV, so I watched a movie from the comfort of the back seat. Eventually, I passed out sleep. Hours later, I was awakened when Connor and Kevin returned to the car after the game. They both looked at me in my dumb-minded state and laughed hysterically. Following the laughs, we decided to fulfill our aftereffects of marijuana (also known as "the munchies"). So, we went to Hooters to eat chicken wings. Those were the best chicken wings I'd ever tasted in my life! It was a day that I will never forget, and one that many of my baseball buddies still tease me about.

While in Scottsdale, Anthony Gwynn Jr. would often invite me to hit with his father, Tony Gwynn. Tony Gwynn was a Major League Baseball Hall of Fame player for the San Diego Padres. In 1999, Tony Gwynn became one of only twenty-two players in baseball history at that time with 3,000 hits. Tony Gwynn was very involved in his son's career and would attend our games regularly. One early morning before a home game, I took Anthony up on his invitation to hit with his father. I walked with Anthony out to the batting cages to get some personal instruction from Mr. Gwynn. The batting cages were located behind the right field fence. When we arrived, Mr. Gwynn was standing in anticipation of his son's arrival. I introduced myself to Mr. Gwynn, and then we got straight to work. I was honored to receive instruction from a Hall of Fame player. I wanted to soak up all the information about hitting as possible. But some of the hitting concepts that were familiar to Anthony, were difficult for me to grasp. Following our workout that day, I was invited by Mr. Gwynn to workout in San Diego, California in the off-season. I could tell that Anthony wanted me to fully understand his father's approach to hitting, which couldn't be done in a one-hour session. I jumped at the opportunity to work with Tony Gwynn and flew out to San Diego in early January of 2006.

When I arrived in San Diego, I was excited to be back in California. Although I was far away from the Bay Area, it felt good to feel the warm Southern California sunshine. While I was in San Diego, I lived with Anthony on the bottom level of his duplex apartment on the beach. Known for its popular Taco Tuesdays, Mission Beach was a popular spot for nightlife. The neighborhood was flooded with beach-goers and bar hoppers on a daily basis. For about a month, I worked out at San Diego State University with about seven other players. Major League Baseball players like Jacques Jones (Minnesota Twins) and Mark Kotsay (Oakland Athletics) were amongst the select group of players seeking hitting instruction from Tony Gwynn. For the first two weeks, we hit whiffle balls in the batting cages. Hitting whiffle balls with Tony Gwynn reminded me of my time spent at the Boys & Girls Club. After cage work, we transitioned to hitting batting practice on the field. We hit multiple rounds of batting practice a day at San Diego State University.

Mr. Gwynn was all work, no play. He only dedicated his time to players who were serious about baseball. My time spent with Mr. Gwynn was priceless. He was the first person to teach me the dynamics of a baseball swing. He pointed out the areas of strength in my swing, which allowed me to recognize which pitches I personally struggled to hit. He explained in detail how to hit the same pitches that had troubled me so much in Round Rock. With this knowledge, I now had an understanding of what I wanted to do at the plate. I knew how to adjust my approach in order to increase my chances for success. Having complete knowledge of my swing was the most important building block of my baseball development. Tony Gwynn helped me grow as a person as well. He challenged me to change the way I perceived both life and baseball. I got the feeling that he wanted me to use my God-given talent, and stop allowing my troubled upbringing to hinder my success. Prior to his passing, Tony Gwynn wrote in a letter:

> *"When I first met CJ, he was a very guarded kid. You could tell that he didn't trust me right away...I told CJ the same thing I've always said to young hitters...keep it simple...He came out and let me tell you, he worked, they all worked. We had 6 or 7 guys working at their craft...But CJ, he really took the information and ran with it. Within a week, he was really starting to trust what he was doing. He really started having some confidence... But CJ was the biggest challenge because like I said 'trust' you had to earn his trust first. Once you did and he saw you were trying to help, he just opened up...I just wanted to help, he did all the rest. Congrats Charlton, you've done quite well my friend."*
> *-Tony Gwynn*

In February, I took my renewed swing to spring training. Back in Major League camp for the second straight year, I was ready to impress. My swing was improved because I was using what Tony Gwynn had taught me. I finally had an idea of what pitch I wanted to hit, and how to approach my at-bats. Prior to hitting with Tony Gwynn, I often couldn't make an adjustment during the at-bat. I now had the ability to make adjustments from pitch-to-pitch. The Houston Astros staff immediately took notice, and wondered who I had worked with during the off-season. Unfortunately, my at-bats were cut short (3-10) to make way for a rising star. Luke Scott was having an unbelievable spring training, and talks of him making the Houston Astros roster began to surface. Major League all-star slugger Lance Berkman underwent orthoscopic knee surgery in 2004, and was questionable for being ready for the Houston Astros 2005 season opener. Luke Scott was quickly becoming the lead candidate to fill that open roster spot if Berkman was not healthy.

MAJOR LEAGUE SPRING TRAINING

After just a few weeks of camp, new Astros manager Phil Garner called me into his office. Again, no player wants to have a one-on-one meeting with

103

a coach! In his office, Garner told me that with the injury to Lance Berkman, the team desperately needed a left-handed bat. Lance Berkman was a switch-hitter (both right and left-handed), but the Astros already had plenty of right-handed hitters on the roster. With that said, Luke Scott would most likely be the person to fill that void. Therefore, I was sent down to Minor League camp in order to prepare for the upcoming season.

Minor League spring training was a bit more *colorful* in 2005. Dave Clark, a former Major League outfielder, was now the manager of the Corpus Christi Hooks. Dave Clark played over a decade of Major League baseball with multiple organizations, including the Pittsburgh Pirates and the Houston Astros. The Corpus Christi Hooks were the new Double-A af-filiate of the Houston Astros in 2005. The Round Rock Express moved up a level to become the new Triple-A affiliate of the Houston Astros. Located in Corpus Christi, Texas, the Hooks were in baseball country. The people of this town loved their baseball and fully supported their local high school baseball teams.

Dave Clark, or "Clarky," managed the Hickory Crawdads in the Carolina League when I played for the Lexington Legends. Back then, I admired his intensity as a coach from afar, and now he was with us. Having Dave Clark around made spring training more enjoyable. Though I wanted to advance to Triple-A, I didn't want to deal with Jackie Moore for another season. I was still hurt by what transpired in the playoffs the year before. The thought of being coached by Dave Clark got me excited about the possibility of repeating the Double-A level. Plus, Clarky would be the second Black manager that I would play for in my entire baseball career. Turns out, the Astros were thinking re-peat as well, but for different reasons. They wanted me to complete another season at the Double-A level so I could figure out what I had been doing wrong the year before. When the final rosters were posted, my name was inked to play for the Corpus Christi Hooks.

Located about 220 miles south of Houston, Corpus Christi is a water-front town with United States military ties. It is the home of the Naval Air Station Corpus Christi, and the legendary battleship USS Lexington. It is also the birthplace of actress Eva Longoria and the late Tejano musician Selena. A coastal city, Corpus Christi is a short drive from the popular spring break tourist city of South Padre Island. Whataburger Field, the Hooks home stadium, was sponsored by the historic Whataburger hamburger restaurant founded in Corpus Christi.

Dave Clark manned his staff with first-year hitting coach John Tamargo Jr., and pitching coach Joe Slusarski. I guess Slusarski followed me from Round Rock to Corpus Christi. Although I wasn't in Round Rock playing Triple-A baseball, I was excited be a part of something new. However, my mental outlook going into the season caused some early offensive struggles. I thought that just because I had already played in the Texas League, I would dominate in my second year. What I didn't take in consideration was the fact that opposing Texas League teams knew me far too well. All the teams kept notes on me from the 2004 season, so they already knew I had a tendency to swing at bad pitches. Therefore, teams pitched to me the same way they did in 2004. I thought I had a new plan and approach, but I was still victim to the same mistakes at the plate. It didn't matter how great my swing was when I continued to swing at balls out of the strike zone. Once again, I piled up too many strikeouts in a hitter-friendly ballpark.

To make matters worse, our team got off to a slow start to our inaugural season as well. We lost twelve of our first twenty games, and the fans were already starting to lose their patience with the team. The only supporters I had through the first month of the season, were the seagulls that swarmed the outfield grass every game. I felt like the seagulls had faith in me, even though I wasn't producing as much as the fans expected. To drown my misery away, I frequented the nightclubs in downtown Corpus Christi. The town was flooded with beautiful women. I called home and told my boys from the Hoop Squad about Corpus Christi. Months later, they all flew down to visit me and support me through my tough season. I booked them a room at a beautiful Corpus Christi beachfront hotel near downtown. For four nights in a row, we went to the club and partied like rock stars. At that time, Darrell was a notable TV personality on MTV Real World/Road Rules Challenge. And Armond had just finished playing basketball at Texas A&M Corpus Christi. There was women swarming around the hotel, eager to hang out with my California crew. Although I was partying a lot, I played much better with the comfort of my boys from back home. Their presence pushed my performance on the field in the right direction. Sometimes, all you need is the support of your family and friends to get you on the right path.

Midway through the season, I hurt my wrist diving for a ball in right field. The team flew me out to Houston to be evaluated by the Houston Astros team doctors. I stayed in Houston for a couple of days so I could be medically evaluated by a hand specialist. They found no broken bones in my hand or wrist, so I returned to Corpus Christi to begin rehabilitation. After being out for about a week, I returned to the lineup. But my wrist still bothered me every game. I continued to play with the pain, even though it killed me every time I swung the bat. In between swings, I hid my grimace of pain by stepping out of the batter's box with my head down. I tried to take as much time as I could to give the pain time to subside before taking yet another painful swing. I couldn't shake the pain, but I also didn't want to be sidelined for weeks with an injury. I knew that I had a good chance of playing in the Major Leagues that year, but I also knew I couldn't do it if I was injured. To help reduce the pain, I spent many hours getting treatment in the training room each day. Before each game, the medical trainer would tape my wrist to provide support. After the game, my wrist was wrapped in ice for about thirty minutes to reduce the swelling. And each day I swallowed as many Aleve pain relievers as I was medically allowed. Not to mention taking other player's prescription Vicodin or Percocet pain killers, whenever I could get my hands on some. From my experience that season, I sympathize with players who become addicted to pain killers. While injured, taking pills to subdue the pain becomes a part of your everyday routine, thus essentially creating a drug habit. This habit can persist long after the injury has been healed. Fortunately, I did not become dependent on pain medication.

For many reasons, I could not wait for the all-star break to arrive. I needed time to rest and to heal my hand. I also needed a break from the game. The break provided time for me to refocus on my goal, which was making it to the Major Leagues. For the three-day break, Mike and I went back to Round Rock to relax. Although we were off for all-star break, the Round Rock Express were busy playing home games at Dell Diamond. Some of my ex-teammates from 2004 were back in Round Rock playing Triple-A baseball for the Express. I was excited go back to Round Rock and see some old faces. Although I didn't want to play there, I still loved being around the folks in Round Rock.

There was a special group of people that I eagerly wanted to see again. Judy Harris and her affectionate family opened their home to the Express baseball players every season. In 2004, Brooks Conrad, Jared Gothreaux, and Mike Rodriguez all lived at the Harris residence. During the season, I spent a lot of time hanging out with Mike at their house. There were at least five Express players at their home on a daily basis when the team was in town. We ate food, played video games, and watched television at the Harris' household. Not only was Judy Harris the matriarch of the household, she was also like a mother to many of the Express players. Judy captured my heart and my stomach with her amazing dessert called "Pinch-Me-Cake." Similar to monkey bread, this cinnamon-sugar laced dessert was like heaven to my taste buds. In fact, just the sight of Pinch-Me-Cake in the cake holder made me happy because it reminded me of grandma's house. Being at the Harris' household allowed me to feel like I was part of a loving home. Something I had always longed for as a child.

Mike and I enjoyed every minute of our return to Round Rock. We went out to the local bars and clubs at night, and floated on inner tubes down the Guadalupe River during the day. My mind was completely free of baseball and the constricting chokehold it had on my life. Because of the liberation I felt in Round Rock, I returned to Corpus Christi with a free mind and a refueled body. I opened the second half of the season on a tear, hitting everything that was pitched. The home runs started flying, the stolen bases started piling up, and I was finally starting to play up to my potential. Looking back, I can clearly see now that Clarky never doubted me at any time during my early struggles. He would always tell me to just relax and have some fun playing the game of baseball. He reminded me daily to not worry about the statistics, or about being called up to the Major Leagues. He said that all I needed to do was prepare for each game. If I was prepared and played hard, good things would happen. He could not have been more right about the future.

TAKING ONE AWAY AT THE WALL IN CORPUS CHRISTI, TEXAS

After continuing to tear up the Texas League competition during second half, I was promoted to Triple-A Round Rock. Since it was the final week of the Express season, many of the Express players had already been called up to play in Houston. Therefore, the Round Rock Express replaced those Triple-A players with players from Corpus Christi and Salem. Charles Gibson, a veteran outfielder for the Express, had been called up to join the Houston Astros outfield. I was promoted to fill his spot as the starting center fielder for the Express. Jackie Moore had the Express in the Pacific Coast League playoff hunt. But with time running out on the season schedule, the Express needed a miracle to make the playoffs.

I was excited about making my Triple-A debut, even though it came with only seven games left in the season. I played extremely well during my short stint in Triple-A, hitting .304 in 21 at-bats. I enjoyed playing Triple-A baseball in cities such as Albuquerque, New Mexico and Nashville, Tennessee. Since these were cities I had never visited before, I made sure I allowed time to be a tourist. Throughout my career, I loved visiting new places to expose myself to different cultures. I always made time to get out of the hotel and explore the town I was visiting. In Nashville, I went downtown to B.B. Kings and listened to live musicians in the birthplace of country music. And since I was in Tennessee, I had to catch up with my old roommate Derek Wigginton. Derek was only miles from Nashville, so he picked me up from my hotel and took me out for a drink. It was great to hang out with Derek again and reminisce about the old days at Miami.

No matter where you're at, the last game of the any baseball season is always fun to play. With nothing at stake, the game is usually played with most players already thinking about the off-season. Therefore, hitters usually swing at the first pitch of their at-bat in hopes of speeding up the game time. The quicker the game is over, the faster the season is over, the faster players can go home. To entice hitters to swing, pitchers usually throw fastballs every pitch. Although, sometimes it can be entertaining to see a batter be fooled by a nasty curveball or dirty change up. For our last game, Dominican pitcher (and locker room barber) Roberto Giron pitched a gem of a game for the Express. Giron had aspirations of being promoted to the Major Leagues following the season. Unfortunately, before the game Giron was informed that he would not be called up to Houston. Instead of sulking in disappointment, Giron pitched an amazing game. Despite the unwritten rules of the final game of the season, Giron was fantastic on the mound. He was the prime example of how to continue to do your job even when things don't go your way.

Although there was some lobbying by Clarky, the Astros had no interest in promoting me to Houston in 2005. When rosters expanded in September, the Astros packed their team roster with veteran Minor League players. The Houston Astros were chasing a wild card spot in the playoffs. Therefore, they wanted players with prior Major League experience. So after our season ended, I caught an airplane flight home to South Florida. Immediately after I touched down in Florida, my body shut down into off-season mode. Within days, my body ached from the injuries I endured during the season. It felt like my body could sense that baseball season was over, and switched into rest and relaxation mode. My sister called me on the phone a few days later and told me that she still believed I would be called up to Houston. I was infuriated by her absurd comment. There was no way I could get called up when the season was already over. I told her that I was already in off-season mode, and didn't want to touch a baseball for quite some time. But her faith was unshaken. Lanette had a vision that I would be promoted to Houston. She believed my destiny was to play Major League baseball in 2005.

After spending about a week at home, on September 13th, 2005 my cell phone rang. At that moment, I was relaxing in bed watching television. I wasn't interested in talking on the phone. When the phone stopped ringing, I reached over to check the missed call log on my phone. To my surprise, someone had called me from a Houston area code. The only calls I had received from Houston area codes in the past, were calls from the Houston Astros front office. I wondered who was calling and why they were calling me at 11:30 p.m. When I called the number back, a man answered the phone and sounded as if he was expecting my call. He calmly said "Hey Charlton, how you doing?" I didn't recognize the voice on the other side of the phone. In a noticeably confused tone of voice, I responded with a classic one-word answer: "Good." He proceeded to ask me how my family was doing. I told him that they were doing alright. At this point, I began thinking to myself that the person talking on the other side of the phone sounded like Ricky Bennett. Mr. Bennett was recently hired as the Director of Player Development for the Houston Astros in 2005. Mr. Bennett and I had talked before during a few player development meetings to discuss my progress. But what did this guy really want so late at night? I needed him to stop beating around the bush and get to the point! We continued to have small talk, but the anxiety was killing me. Then, he uttered the words that would change the tone of the conversation and change my life. He said, "Well, you made it to the Big Leagues, you're coming to Houston." I instantly told him to stop playing with me. Surely, I could not be called up to Houston from the comfort of my home. Especially not after being idle from playing baseball for nearly a week. But this was no prank call, he was serious. My former teammate Willy Taveras was injured earlier that night during a game in Houston. Therefore, the Astros needed an extra player just in case Taveras would be out for an extended amount of time. In the blink of an eye, I was promoted to the Houston Astros Baseball Club.

After talking with Mr. Bennett, I immediately called my sister and told her the good news. She was ecstatic, but not surprised. She already believed in her heart that this moment would come to pass this year, even when I thought it was impossible. Though not deeply religious, Lanette's unwavering faith in God powered her belief that I would play Major League baseball in 2005. We didn't come from a church-going family, so her faith was built solely on her personal relationship with God.

In the end, all those days of hard work had paid off. I was about to be a part of an elite group of players that were fortunate enough to make it to the Major Leagues. Not to mention an even smaller group of Black players fortunate enough to reach the Major Leagues. Based on the Richard Lapchick's Institute for Diversity and Ethics in Sports report, only 9.0 percent of MLB players were Black to start to 2005 season. That number most likely would not increase by the end of the 2005 season. The odds of making it to the Major Leagues was slim, but not impossible by any means. I had overcome the odds in more ways than one.

On September 14th, 2005, my flight to Houston departed around 9 a.m. Even though I was completely exhausted, I couldn't sleep during my flight to Houston. I usually get some good sleep on plane flights, but this flight was exceptional. I could not stop thinking about the moment when I would don a Major League uniform. After arriving in Houston at about 11 a.m., I caught an airport shuttle to Minute Maid Park. At the ballpark, I met with Houston Astros manager Phil Garner. Garner took over as Astros manager in the middle of the 2004 season after Jimy Williams was fired. Garner didn't talk to me much, and definitely didn't invest his time in me like Jimy Williams did. Therefore, our conversion was brief and without much guidance on what he expected from me to help the team.

Already present in the locker room were a few players and coaches that I hadn't seen since spring training. I greeted them and then promptly searched for the locker labeled with "Jimerson." I eagerly wanted to know which jersey number they had given me. Once I found my locker, my dream of making it to the Major Leagues became reality. Seeing my name in a Major League clubhouse was a snapshot in history that I will never forget. At that moment, I knew I had finally made it. My jersey number was #52, which was ironic since I also wore

#52 at Miami. I went from wearing #52 as a walk-on baseball player at Miami, to wearing #52 as a Major League baseball player for the Houston Astros.

Pitching that night in my first Major League game, was newly acquired superstar Roger Clemens. Arguably the most dominant pitcher of all-time, Clemens had already won seven Cy Young awards, and two World Series rings. Clemens signed an $18 million contract with the Houston Astros in 2005, making him the highest paid pitcher in MLB history at that time. Clemens was essentially a baseball robot, who was willing to do anything to stay above the competition. But on that day, Clemens had a heavy heart since his mother had just passed away. Instead of taking time off to mourn, Clemens courageously took the mound in honor of his late mother. Roger's dedication to both his family and the game of baseball gave him the motivation to pitch. The Astros were in contention for the National League Wild Card. Winning the National League Wild Card would give the Astros a spot in the 2005 MLB playoffs. The Astros desperately needed to win to keep their playoffs chances alive. There was no pitcher better suited to win a Major League baseball game for his team than Roger Clemens.

About an hour before game time, I went to my locker to get dressed in uniform. To my disgust, my baseball pants were not my size. In spring training, all 40-man roster players are measured for their baseball uniform size. Somehow, my measurements must have been misplaced, because the pants I had on could not have been my size in spring training. My baseball pants were like skinny jeans when I preferred a more relaxed fit. There was no way I could fit my big ass in those snug-fit baseball pants. The Astros always told their players, "you can wear your pants however you want…in the Major Leagues." Therefore, I was highly disappointed that my baseball pants were not how I wanted. I notified the guy in charge of uniforms about the obvious miscalculation. In a disrespectful manner, he tossed me a new pair of pants and muttered, "Fucking rookies" as he marched off. I wanted to slap the taste out of his mouth, but that wouldn't have been a great start to my Major League career! Instead, I finished dressing in my uniform, then went out to the field to prepare for the game. I wasn't about to let something like that ruin my grandiose first day in the Major Leagues.

BIG LEAGUE CHEW

Being able to watch a legendary pitcher like Roger Clemens from such close range was a treat. I wasn't just another fan, watching Clemens pitch from a mezzanine level seat. I was his teammate, and we were now in the battle for the playoffs together. Clemens pitched a gem of a game, allowing just one run, on five hits, in six innings against the Florida Marlins. He was simply spectacular as he paid homage to his mother by doing what he does best—pitch. In the top of the ninth inning, the sold-out crowd at Minute Maid Park gave Roger Clemens a standing ovation as he walked off the mound. As he departed, I entered the game to play center field. My run from our team's dugout to the outfield grass felt like slow motion. My feet floated high in the air, and landed ever so softly as they hit the ground. The distance from the dugout to the outfield felt like a mile away.

When I reached the outfield, I glanced back at the scoreboard to catch a glimpse of my name in bright lights. I wanted to mentally capture that moment so that I would never forget it. The feeling of playing in a Major League baseball game was like no other experience in my baseball career. It was truly amazing to see 30,000 fans in their seats watching a game that I was playing in. Though I never appeared in another game that season, I enjoyed every minute of my playing time on that special night.

Being in the Major Leagues was unbelievable. I loved being treated like royalty—eating at 5-star restaurants, staying in the best hotels, and people waiting on me hand and foot. I had no problem getting used to the luxuries of a Major League baseball player. However, I struggled to understand certain standards of being a Major League baseball player. For example, Major Leaguers don't carry their own luggage to their hotel room, they pay a bellman to do it. Major Leaguers don't eat fast food at the local mall, they order expensive room service. And if you're a rookie, the standards are even higher. Rookies can't ride the team bus from the hotel to visiting stadiums, they have to pay for a taxi to take them to games. Rookies can't use an alias name when staying at the team hotels either. For example, Roger Clemens used the name "Kingfish" as his alias to prevent fans from knowing which hotel room he was occupying. And probably the most heinous aspect of being a rookie, is that you have to be initiated into Major League Baseball. Our rookie initiation in 2005 took place in Chicago, Illinois while playing the Chicago Cubs. After the game, I noticed something missing in my locker. The suit and tie I wore to the stadium had been replaced by a women's sundress. When I looked around, several others rookies also had sundresses in their locker. That's when I realized that this was not just some random joke. Our rookie initiation was to wear women's clothing while we travelled to play the St. Louis Cardinals. Therefore, I put on my brown print sundress, dress socks and dress shoes. Players and coaches combined were laughing and taking pictures with their cell phone cameras. There I stood, looking like a NFL defensive end with an Easter Sunday dress on. We had to wear these hideous outfits all the way to St. Louis, Missouri. As we exited the stadium, fans were waiting by the team bus for autographs. They got a good laugh from watching a bunch of professional athletes walking around in dresses. It was all in fun, and I respected the tradition. Besides, I think I looked pretty good in a dress! On our chartered flight, all the rookies served food and drinks to the team wearing our beautiful sundresses. I accepted the humility because I knew it was all part of the life of a Major League baseball player.

MY SUNDRESS AT WRIGLEY FIELD

We clinched the National League Wild Card on the last day of the season by beating the Chicago Cubs 6-4 at Minute Maid Park. After the final out, we celebrated on the field with the classic baseball "dog-pile" on the mound. Subsequent to our on-field celebration, I was called into Phil Garner's office for a meeting. Like I said before, no player wants to have a one-on-one meeting with a coach. In his office, I was notified that I would be leaving Houston. Instead of staying with the team throughout the 2005 playoffs, I was going back to the Arizona Fall League to play for a second straight year. I left Garner's office disappointed that I would not be with the team for the playoffs. To drown my sorrows, I stayed in the clubhouse hours after the game was over, drinking Vodka and grapefruit cocktails with Brad Ausmus and Jeff Bagwell.

The 2005 Houston Astros went on to win the National League Divisional title and play in their first World Series in franchise history. The Chicago White Sox swept the Astros, needing only four games to capture a World Series title. Despite not being with the team for the playoffs, I still received a National League Champion ring. Any player who was on the active Houston Astros roster during the season received a ring as well. Although the ring was immaculate—diamond encrusted Houston Astros star set in ruby—it had little sentimental value. The same feelings I felt my sophomore year at Miami after winning the College World Series resurfaced. Since I only played three total outs for the Houston Astros in 2005, I felt disconnected from their historic season. To this day, I still regret not being with the team while they battled to become Major League Baseball champions. The bittersweet ending to my season made me yearn for another day in the Major Leagues. My time playing in the Major Leagues was far too brief for it to be over. But if I never played another day in the Major Leagues, I was at peace with my baseball career. I recognized that I was extremely blessed to have played Major League baseball, even if it was only for one inning. In my heart, I felt like I belonged in the Major Leagues. All I needed to do was continue to build on what I started in 2005.

9TH INNING:

While preparing for the 2006 season, the only thing on my mind was returning to Houston. Since I only had a "cup of coffee" in the Major Leagues, I believed it was my year to return to Houston and stay. A cup of coffee is a common saying in Major League Baseball. Essentially, a cup of coffee means a player only spent enough time in the Major Leagues to drink a cup of coffee. I wanted more than a cup of coffee, I wanted to hang out in the Major Leagues like I was at Starbucks. My swagger was at an all-time high when I reported to spring training in 2006. I was moving with more confidence because I was a certified Major League baseball player. There was nothing anyone could do to take that away from me. Although I glowed with confidence on the outside, internally I was full of uncertainty. I wasn't sure if I was Major League ready, yet I kept the persona of a player who was undoubtedly ready. I've always been a believer in the phrase "fake it until you make it." In baseball, it means you play the position until it becomes you. Even though I had yet to receive an at-bat in the Major Leagues, I carried myself like I had 100 Major League at-bats already.

I definitely had not accomplished all that I was capable of doing in the Minor Leagues. Therefore, I acknowledged the likelihood of returning to Triple-A to play a full season. I wondered if I had worked hard enough—lifted enough weights, or ran enough sprints to be ready for the 2006 season. So many players use different training regiments to get ready for the season. Some players hire personal trainers, while others work out at professional training facilities. Although I questioned if I was prepared, I always believed that I had enough personal drive to compete with anyone.

The Houston Astros added a new face to the organization with the acquisition of veteran outfielder Preston Wilson. Preston was a player who I admired for years for displaying a deadly combination of speed and power. He also flashed a great glove in the outfield and struggled with striking out. With Preston signed to a one-year, $4 million contract, the Astros made it clear that there was no need for two players with similar tools. After spending just a few weeks in camp with limited at-bats, I was optioned to Minor League spring training.

I wasn't bothered by being sent down to Minor League spring training because I had been down this road twice before. However, this year the Astros Minor League staff treated me unfairly. They were unnecessarily harder on me than other players whom had not played in the Major Leagues. Anytime I made a mistake, they reprimanded me in front of my peers. They wanted to broadcast to everyone that I would not receive preferential treatment solely because I played in Houston in 2005. Despite my unwarranted treatment, I continued to work on my craft during Minor League spring training.

When the 2006 season rosters were set, I found myself back on the Round Rock Express roster. Jackie Moore was still the head coach of the Express, but joining his staff in 2006 were Harry Spilman, and Burt Hooton. Spilman and Hooton were the new hitting and pitching coaches, respectively. Spike Owen remained on the Express coaching staff as third base coach. To my surprise, the Express had an influx of new players acquired via free agency. Veteran players like Joe McEwing, and Alan Zinter were now amongst the many familiar faces in the clubhouse. Both McEwing and Zinter had spent substantial time in the Major Leagues with other organizations. I was interested in getting to know the personalities of all my new teammates.

I could not help but wonder where Jackie would place me in the lineup to begin the 2006 season. The last time I was a member of the Express, Jackie put me eight in the batting order during the 2004 Texas League playoffs. I guess he had an epiphany since losing in the playoffs, because I opened the season hitting leadoff. I was excited about the opportunity to hit leadoff for the Express. As the starting center fielder and leadoff hitter for the Express, my season started off with a bang. By mid-season, I was among the league leaders in extra base hits and stolen bases. I also had nearly twenty home runs, several of which were to lead off the game. It reminded me of my glory days at the University of Miami. I was trying to do damage from the first pitch and wasn't interested in working the count or trying to draw a walk.

As a result of my hitting approach, my strikeouts slowly but surely began to pile on after the all-star break. Overall, I was getting more at-bats each game than the rest of my teammates by hitting leadoff. But the more at-bats I got, the more strikeouts I recorded in my stats. I struck out at least once a game, and nobody was shocked when I struck out multiple times. I thought I had matured past swinging and missing since becoming more knowledgeable of my swing. But no matter how much my swing had improved, nobody could hit some of the pitches I was swinging at. In baseball, sometimes is better to simply stop swinging, and allow the pitcher to throw you strikes. But, you have to swallow your pride and be patient enough to let some good pitches go by.

Since I was both striking out and smashing home runs at the same time, I had an important decision to make. Either start cutting down on my strikeouts, or to continue to let the bat fly. Even though I was striking out in bunches, I was putting up some big numbers in other offensive categories. Therefore, I chose to continue to let it fly. My decision ultimately caused Jackie to move me down to eighth in the lineup for the remainder of the season. Just like in the 2004 playoffs, I was furious about the move. Even though I was striking out a lot, I was getting a lot of big hits at key moments of games for our team. After being moved to the bottom of the lineup, my overall production naturally decreased. My offensive numbers plummeted at an alarming rate. I went from being one of the top five players in the league in runs scored, to just mediocre. I also fell behind on the leaderboard in stolen bases. Each day my name was listed in the eighth spot, Jackie was diverting my talent from being an asset to the team. I felt like he was trying to show me who was boss. In response, I made it my mission every day to show him that I controlled my own destiny. Apparently, that only made him search for new ways to impose his position.

One day in Colorado Springs, Colorado, Jackie Moore enforced his authority in a big way. The Colorado Sky Sox were the 2006 Triple-A affiliate of the Colorado Rockies. The Express and Sky Sox played a compelling game in horrible cold and rainy weather conditions. In the game, I already had two hits in three at-bats, before preparing for my fourth at-bat. With the bases loaded, one out, and down one run in the eighth inning, I was excited to hit. I always welcomed the opportunity to drive in some runs and put my team ahead. However, instead of allowing me to hit, Jackie called me back to the bench. Infielder Joe McEwing strolled towards the plate to pinch-hit in my spot. I returned to the dugout in total confusion and disbelief that I was being taken out of the game at such a critical moment. I watched from the bench as Joe McEwing proceeded to take my at-bat. McEwing hit into an inning-ending double play, which abruptly ended our scoring threat. I was disappointed that Jackie didn't believe in me to produce for our team. I shouldn't have been surprised by his actions, for he had shown me what he was capable of back in 2004.

Since I could not re-enter the game—based on the rules—I wanted to change my wet undergarments. I had played in the pouring rain for over three hours, so I desperately wanted some dry clothes. After changing garments, I intended to return to our dugout to watch the final inning of the game. In between innings, I grabbed my equipment and headed up to the clubhouse. A rather unique stadium, Security Service Field built its visiting locker room above the concourse. Therefore, in order to get to our clubhouse, I had to escalate up the stadium stairs. When I arrived in the clubhouse, many of our pitchers were already inside. Some of them had pitched earlier in the game, so by rule, they also could not re-enter the game. Others were just hanging out in the clubhouse, doing nothing of importance. In baseball, it is common practice for players to grab a snack or a hot cup of coffee in the clubhouse between innings.

Being amongst the other players, I guess I got comfortable inside our warm clubhouse. The clubhouse had a television channel playing a live broadcast of our ongoing game. I believe that the channel had been set up to allow players in the clubhouse the ability to see the action on the field. It was a convenient way of knowing what was happening in the game in real-time. It allowed players to properly gauge when they needed to be back on the field. I watched the game for a few outs, and before I realize it, the game was over. The Sky Sox scored the game winning run in the bottom of the ninth inning. I waited by my locker for the other players to reach the clubhouse from the field. After a loss, it's deemed disrespectful to be already showering or eating the post-game dinner before the other players arrive. Besides, each player should designate time after a loss to evaluate how they personally factored into losing the game. As players and coaches flooded into the clubhouse, I could tell by the look on the faces of my teammates that something was wrong. One by one, players entered the clubhouse and scanned the room. It was obvious to me that they wanted to make eye contact with the players who were inside the clubhouse during the game.

Within seconds, Jackie called everyone's attention and initiated a team meeting. After speaking for less than thirty seconds, Jackie surprisingly uttered my name. He claimed that I specifically abandoned my teammates and left them out on the field while they battled to win. He accused me of returning to the clubhouse in haste because I was upset about being pinch-hit for. I was disturbed by the accusations and how I was being portrayed to my teammates. I wasn't angry that McEwing pinch-hit in my place. I always respected McEwing and his accomplished Major League career with the St. Louis Cardinals and New York Mets. I might have been a little disappointed, but the purpose of going to the clubhouse was to change my clothes. I could not believe that the basis of the meeting was to designate me as the culprit.

Immediately after Jackie finished speaking his misguided words, I seized the opportunity to express my displeasure with being singled out. I did not want his perception of my actions to become the perception of my peers. How my teammates viewed me, not Jackie Moore, meant the most to me. I spoke out and told him that I wasn't the only player in the clubhouse while the game was being played. And for that matter, players are frequently in the clubhouse during games. I questioned what made my actions so different on that day. He had no response to my question, and appeared to be baffled by my speaking out. He ended the meeting by declaring a new rule: no players in the clubhouse during the game.

Later that night, many of my teammates joked about what transpired during our team meeting. However, several players believed that I responded in a disrespectful manner by speaking out. In their collective opinion, in was not my place to voice my intentions. I needed to keep quiet and allow Jackie to conduct our team meeting. I appreciated their opinion, but I would never sit back and be quiet while another man makes false accusations about me. Besides, these types of problems occur every year on plenty of professional baseball teams. I figured this was an isolated incident that would be water under the bridge going forward.

Minutes after I arrived at the clubhouse the next day, Jackie Moore abruptly called me into his office. When I entered his office, Spike Owen and Harry Spilman were already inside sitting down. Jackie was sitting behind his desk, with a stack of papers in his hand. Jackie opened the meeting by informing me that I was suspended three games without pay for my actions the previous night. He cited the Houston Astros Player Code of Conduct as the reason for my suspension. He stated a player could be penalized for three days without pay for unsportsmanlike conduct. I was in total disbelief about what was going on. Was he seriously suspending me for unsportsmanlike conduct? This is why a player never wants to be in a one-on-one meeting. Unexpected ambush suspensions can occur!

When Jackie handed me the suspension papers to sign, I crumbled the papers up and shouted numerous profanities with all my breath. I was furious because my suspension had already been endorsed by the Astros. I was never provided the opportunity to explain my intentions. Most baseball managers will give a player a chance to justify their actions before rushing to judgment. Jackie had no interest in hearing my reasoning, his perception was reality. Spike and Harry watched in silence as I stormed out of the office and kicked over a garbage can as I exited the clubhouse. I paced around the stadium parking lot for nearly an hour, trying to comprehend what just occurred. I felt helpless that I could not appeal the suspension. I have never accepted being helpless in my life.

Since no one else was suspended for being inside the clubhouse, my suspension was essentially exile from the team. For the next three games, I sat by myself and watched from the stands while my team played. Even after returning from my suspension, I didn't play for four more games due to an "unofficial suspension." My good friend and teammate Humberto Quintero believed I would continue to not play unless I apologized to the team. Therefore, I approached Jackie Moore and asked him for his approval to hold another team meeting. With Jackie's consent, all Express players gathered on August 9th, 2006 in Salt Lake City, Utah. We were on the road playing against the Salt Lake City Bees, 2006 Triple-A affiliate of the Los Angeles Angels. Jackie stood in the corner of the room, observing and listening from afar. However, Spike Owen and Harry Spilman purposely did not attend the meeting. I stood tall in the middle of the room and apologized to each player and coach for my actions. I expressed to them how bad I felt about what transpired in Colorado Springs. My voice trembled with emotion—I wanted my teammates to feel the sincerity in my words.

Unfortunately, my apology opened the door for a select group of players to criticize me during the meeting. They complained about the manner in which I went about my business. Instead of accepting my apology, they attacked my character as a person. Listening to their comments caused my mind to drift and my body to feel numb to emotions. At that moment, I realized that none of my teammates truly knew my character except for Mike Rodriguez. In all my years of playing baseball, I never before had any problems of this magnitude with my teammates. All of sudden, I was viewed as the problem child of the team. I believe they conspired to show their loyalty to Jackie by perpetuating the conflict instead of resolving it.

The treatment I received during my suspension only intensified my desire to play the game of baseball. Not only was I playing against the opposing team, but I was also playing to prove my teammates and coaches wrong. I felt totally disrespected by coaches Harry Spilman and Spike Owen for intentionally not attending my meeting. When I returned playing baseball, Harry Spilman refused to work with me in the batting cages before games. He also never provided instruction concerning my at-bats during the games. Basically, Harry Spilman attempted to ostracize me from the team. To piss him off, I worked in the batting cages by myself before every game. And when the lights came on, I dominated opposing pitchers game after game. Spike Owen continued to act in a contemptuous manner, by refusing to give me a high five whenever I rounded third base on a home run. He always gave his players a congratulatory high five when rounding third base on a home run. His refusal to slap hands when I rounded third base was blatant disrespect. I kept hitting home runs so I could keep irritating Spike Owen every time I came around third base.

TEARING IT UP IN ROUND ROCK WITH MY SPEED, POWER, AND DEFENSE

It didn't matter what they tried to do to me because my mind was set on the Major Leagues. No one on the Round Rock Express coaching staff could stop me from returning to the Major Leagues. Where I was headed didn't include Jackie Moore, Harry Spilman, or Spike Owen. Triple-A is a level where coaches see players advance to the Major Leagues all year long while they remain. How I responded to their actions was the only thing that could prevent me from returning to Houston. I had been through way too much in my life to let them stop me from reaching my destiny.

On August 31st, 2006, I was called into Jackie's office for the first time since the incident in Colorado. Still uncomfortable about one-on-one meetings with coaches, I reluctantly entered his office. This time Jackie shook my hand, and told me that I would be leaving for Houston the following day. It was a bittersweet moment to say the least. I was excited about returning to the Major Leagues, but I was saddened by the recently soiled relationship between me and Jackie. I thanked him for all that he had done to help me get back to Houston. I had an intuition that Jackie never intended for our relationship to sour. I believe that he was coerced by his assistant coaches to act with malice following the game in Colorado Springs. I will never forget the day Jackie told me I was going to the Major Leagues. It was a moment that I longed for since leaving Houston in 2005.

Preparing for my travel to Houston in 2006 was a lot calmer than the first time. I was able to pack up my belongings in my truck, and drive the three-hour trip from Round Rock. When I arrived at Minute Maid Park, I knew exactly how to navigate to the Astros clubhouse since I was in Houston the year before. I was happy to see my #52 jersey and a pair of baseball pants that actually fit my measurements, hanging in my locker. Everything was perfectly laid out for me this time around. Although I felt a sense of belonging, I acknowledged my limits of comfort. I understood that playing Major League baseball was a privilege. In the blink of an eye, my Major League status could be snatched away, and without reason.

The 2006 Astros were in playoff contention, competing for the National League Wild Card. Before the game, manager Phil Garner told me to be ready to pinch run or play defense at any time. But what I wanted to hear him say was to have my bat ready to hit at any time. I still had not recorded a Major League at-bat in my career. I worked hard to improve my swing since my Major League debut in 2005. I absolutely could not wait to show off my skills in a game.

The Astros were ranked near the cellar in team batting average all year long. Preston Wilson was no longer with the club, Jeff Bagwell was battling a shoulder injury, and Craig Biggio was on the brink of retirement. Therefore, the Astros depended on the bat of Lance Berkman for offense. Berkman was having an historic season, setting Houston Astros single season records in both home runs and RBIs. The Astros pitching staff was among the best in the league. The starting rotation consisted of three all-star pitchers in Roger Clemens, Andy Pettitte, and Roy Oswalt. Not to mention one of the best closers in the game in Brad Lidge.

My first series after joining the team was at home against the New York Mets. I sat on the bench all three games against the Mets, as we lost two out of three games at Minute Maid Park. At that time, I already began to doubt that Houston would give me substantial playing time in the Major Leagues. Judging by the overall lack of offensive production, I could not see why the Astros staff did not already give me a chance to play. I wanted to show the world that I could play at the highest level.

Our next nine games were on the road against the Philadelphia Phillies (3 games), Milwaukee Brewers (3 games), and the St. Louis Cardinals (3 games). On September 4th, 2006, Roger Clemens got the nod to pitch in the Labor Day game against the Phillies. Taking the mound for the Phillies was lefty ace Cole Hamels. The game in Philadelphia started as a typical National League battle, with neither offense doing much damage. In the fifth inning, Philadelphia held on to a 1-0 lead while Hamels breezed through our lineup. In fact, Hamels was perfect through five innings, allowing no hits and no runs while striking out seven. In the middle of the fifth inning, bench coach Cecil Cooper told me to start getting loose. Finally, I was going to get a chance to pinch run or play defense as Garner had aforementioned. I went down the stairs of our dugout, and underneath the stadium concourse. I began to stretch out and get loose within the tunnel connecting the visiting clubhouse to the visiting dugout. Meanwhile, Clemens went back on the mound for the bottom of the fifth and pitched a scoreless inning. But after recording the last out of inning, Clemens walked off the mound in obvious physical discomfort. He appeared to have injured his groin throwing to the last Phillies hitter he faced.

In the dugout, the Astros medical trainer hovered over Clemens trying to determine the severity of his injury. Clemens didn't feel physically well enough to continue pitching in the game. His spot in the lineup was coming up third in Astros half of the sixth inning. Therefore, someone would need to hit for Clemens since he was unable to continue playing. Cecil Cooper walked down to where I was warming up and told me to get ready to hit. He said I would hit for Clemens if there were two outs and nobody on base when his spot in the lineup came up.

I rushed to grab my batting gloves and my bat so I could be ready to hit. Selfishly, I waited and hoped that the first two batters made outs. Astros short-stop Adam Everett led off the top of the sixth inning with a line drive out to left field…**ONE OUT**. Up next, was catcher and fan favorite Brad Ausmus. As he strolled to the plate, I headed towards the on-deck batting circle. The excitement over the possibility of finally getting an at-bat caused my breathing to become irregular. I had to repeatedly remind myself to relax and breath. I could feel the eyes of thousands of fans peering down at me while I prepared to hit. I went through my regular on-deck circle routine—put the bat weight on my bat, twirl the bat over my head, and take three practice swings. As I prepared to hit, my mind went completely blank as I stared out towards the mound at Cole Hamels. I suddenly forgot about all the people in the stadium, and focused solely on the pitcher.

After two or three pitches were thrown to Ausmus, I snapped out my daze. I began thinking about what my plan would be at the plate if I got a chance to hit. I knew Hamels had a good fastball and a nasty changeup, so I watched closely what he threw to Ausmus. On the fourth pitch from Hamels, Brad Ausmus hit a flare down the right field line. As soon as the ball was hit, I thought for sure it would drop behind first base for a hit. My hope for getting my first Major League at-bat began to fade as the ball traveled towards right field. Luckily, Phillies second baseman Chase Utley ran it down and made a spectacular over the shoulder catch…**TWO OUTS**.

It was finally my chance to hit. But before I proceeded to home plate, I took one last glance back at Phil Garner. I needed to be certain that I was hitting to avoid a monumental let down. Phil Garner gave me a head nod of assurance, and I made my way towards home plate. I felt like Mike Tyson on his way into the ring before a heavyweight title bout. My walk was slow and calculated, with hint of confidence in each stride. I don't know if I was prepared for the moment, but I had definitely been through enough in my life to handle the moment. My childhood had taught me how to maneuver in the midst of pressure situations.

When I reached the batter's box, my primary focus was to avoid embarrass myself. I acknowledged that there were people watching from their seats, as well as those watching from their television. Since it was my first at-bat, I decided to impersonate the Major League players that I had watched on television. I said hello to both Phillies catcher Chris Coste, and home plate umpire Joe West. They reciprocated my greeting, then Mr. West made notation in his official scorecard that I was pinch-hitting for Clemens.

From my field of vision, Cole Hamels gleamed with confidence from the mound. At that juncture, Hamels was pitching a perfect game and a no-hitter. In baseball, a "perfect game" is when a pitcher doesn't allow an opposing hitter to reach base in any fashion. A "no-hitter" is when a pitcher doesn't allow a hit, yet an opposing hitter has reached base. A no-hitter remains intact even if an opposing hitter reaches base via an error or walk. Cole Hamels had retired all seventeen Astros hitters that he faced. Therefore, there was more at stake in the game for Hamels than just getting the win.

Hamels eagerly awaited his next challenger—Charlton Maxwell Jimerson— a rookie who had yet to record a Major League at-bat. As usual, I went through my routine before hitting. I made my spot in the batter's box by digging a foot hole with my cleats. Then, I kicked the dirt in the batter's box around a little, before using my bat to knock the excess dirt off my cleats. Lastly, I scanned the playing field to see where the defense was positioned. I took a deep breath, and stepped into the batter's box ready to hit.

Without hesitation, Cole Hamels wound up and threw a fastball for ball one. I was surprised the pitch was called a ball because it would have been called a strike every time in the Minor Leagues. I stepped out and took another deep breath. Then I stepped back in the batter's box and waited for Hamels' second pitch. It was another fastball that was called a ball yet again by the umpire.

At this point, I started feeling good about my at-bat. It seemed like Hamels had to throw it right over the middle of the plate for the pitch to be called a strike. I stepped out again and got ready to hit the next pitch. Since the count was in my favor at two balls and no strikes, I was looking for a pitch I could crush. When I stepped back in to hit, Hamels reared back and threw a changeup for strike one. I had no clue why I didn't attempt to swing at the pitch. Every bone in my body was geared to swing at that 2-0 pitch, but instead I watched it pass by. For some odd reason, when I stepped out of the batter's box, I felt good about my at-bat. Because I failed to swing at the first three pitches, it gave the impression to my coaches and teammates that I was patiently looking for one particular pitch. For once in my career, I was displaying discipline at the plate without even trying!

I took another deep breath, and told myself to swing at the next pitch if it was in the strike zone. I didn't want to watch two strikes go by without swinging. Besides, you can't get a hit if you never swing. I stepped back in the batter's box and awaited Hamels' next offering. Cole Hamels started his wind up, reeled back, and threw another changeup. My eyes got big as the familiar pitch approached me. When it got into the hitting zone, I swung and heard a loud pop. By the feeling in my hands on the bat when I made contact, I knew I had hit it a long way. When I looked up to locate the ball, it was rocketing towards the center field wall. I sprinted towards first base, and right before I reached first base, I looked up again. The ball soared over the center field wall at Citizen's Bank Park, and nearly hit a camera man when it landed. I just hit a home run in my first Major League at bat!

I jogged around the bases like a colt with unstable legs. I had hit many home runs in my baseball career, but never before in a Major League baseball game. When I touched home plate, Craig Biggio was standing there to greet me as he waited his turn to hit next. I headed towards the dugout and Willy Taveras was jumping up and down on the top step. He might have been happier about my home run than I was. When I got to the dugout, I gave high fives to every teammate, coach, and trainer as I walked through the dugout. Everyone was extremely congratulatory and genuinely happy for me. The crowd was stunned with disbelief about what I had just done. The Phillies lead was gone, and Cole

Hamels' perfect game and no-hit bid was wiped away in one swing. To show their appreciation and love for the game of baseball, Phillies fans applauded my home run. Even though I played for the opposing team, they understood that something special just occurred. At that time, only 94 players in Major League history had hit a home run in their first Major League at-bat. As a token of respect, a fan threw my home run ball back on the field. Phillies center fielder Shane Victorino grabbed the ball, and tossed it towards the dugout so that I can keep the ball for memories.

Following the greatest moment of my baseball career, I had the biggest smile on my face. For the next 30 minutes, I sat on the bench and replayed the home run in my head. But as the game progressed, I gradually zoned out from baseball and began thinking about life. On that sunny day in Philadelphia, I realized that my success in life was bigger than baseball. Baseball was simply my stage to display my achievements, but my success was not solely based on baseball statistics. I reflected with pride on how far I had come to arrive at this moment. Not measured by miles, but rather by the many obstacles I had overcome to be successful in life. Surviving a broken home, avoiding drug addiction and alcoholism, and resisting the temptations of fast money, were all greater accomplishments than home runs. Receiving higher education (and later completing my Bachelor of Science degree in Computer Science), would prove to be far more rewarding than any baseball game I'd ever played in. Against all odds, I became successful in life. And that is something I will always remember.

ACKNOWLEDGMENTS

This book highlighting my unbelievable journey through life would have never come to fruition without the help of so many people along the way. Special thanks to Lisa Winston and Sarah Cortez for all that you did. This project could not have been completed without the assistance of you two wonderful women. Throughout my life, I have met so many great people across multiple countries. I have learned something from each and every one of you all. Special shout out to Ted Muniz, Alex Sanders, Darrell Taylor, Alfred Dyer, Armond Wainright, Doug Lymon, Mike Rodriguez, Darryl Roque, Marcus Nettles, Greg Lovelady, Jamin Thompson, Rashawn Grogans, Roy McCoy, Kalee Jaimah, Kiri Seliger, Krystin Edwards, Tommy Whiteman, Cameron Likely, Fehlandt Lentini, Judy Harris, Chuck Carlson, Jim Morris, Gino DiMare, Lazer Collazo, Turtle Thomas, and Mark Kingston.

To my lovely sister, only God knows how much you have sacrificed for me. You are the most loving woman on God's green earth. Thank you so much for the guidance along the way. To my beautiful children Alexa, Tyson, Nicolas and Carter, Daddy loves you more than life itself. Thank you so much Mrs. Candace "Sweet P" Jimerson for putting up with me and seeing my vision through. You already have plans for the next book! Thank you to the University of Miami for giving me the opportunity for higher education. Go 'Canes!!! To the cities of Houston, TX, Kissimmee, FL, Pittsfield, MA, Lexington, KY, Salem, VA, Round Rock, TX, Corpus Christi, TX, Scottsdale, AZ, and Surprise, AZ, thank you for your hospitality.

"This be the realest shit I ever wrote, against all odds"
–Tupac Shakur

Photos provided by: ProCanes and Omaha Herald

22137210R00079

Made in the USA
San Bernardino, CA
21 June 2015